Socratic Seminars in Middle School

Teach students how to engage in thoughtful discussions about a text. Socratic seminars are highly effective at helping students read closely and think critically about what they've read. They also teach students how to participate in authentic discussions. This practical book from bestselling authors Victor and Marc Moeller is your go-to guide for getting started! It will help teachers who are new at Socratic seminars and provide fresh ideas to teachers who are experienced with the format. Part I provides guidelines on how to prepare students for discussion and how to form good discussion questions. Part II includes ready-to-use lesson plans organized by compelling themes to engage students. The lesson plans include unabridged literary and nonfiction reading selections from classic and contemporary authors, as well as suggested film pairings.

Authors featured in this book include . . .

- William Faulkner
- Gina Berriault
- Gene Siskel
- President Obama
- Ray Bradbury
- Kurt Vonnegut, Jr.
- Khalil Gibran
- William Shakespeare
- Robert Frost
- William Saroyan
- Carson McCullers
- And more!

Victor J. Moeller is an English professor at McHenry Community College in Illinois.

Marc V. Moeller teaches English at Prairie Middle School in the Barrington Community Unit School District in Illinois.

Socratic Seminars in Middle School

Text and Films That Engage Students in Reflective Thinking and Close Reading

Victor J. Moeller and Marc V. Moeller

Routledge
Taylor & Francis Group
NEW YORK AND LONDON

First published 2015
by Routledge
711 Third Avenue, New York, NY 10017

and by Routledge
2 Park Square, Milton Park, Abingdon, Oxon, OX14 4RN

Routledge is an imprint of the Taylor & Francis Group, an informa business

Sections of this book were previously published as *Socratic Seminars and Literature Circles*, © 2001.

Library of Congress Cataloging-in-Publication Data
Moeller, Victor J., 1937–
Socratic seminars in middle school : texts and films that engage students in reflective thinking and close reading / Victor Moeller, Marc Moeller.
pages cm
Includes bibliographical references and index.
1. Questioning. 2. Literature—Study and teaching (Middle school)
I. Moeller, Marc V., 1970– II. Title.
LB1027.44M643 2014
371.3′7—dc23
2014007666

ISBN: 978-1-138-02321-5 (hbk)
ISBN: 978-1-138-02322-2 (pbk)
ISBN: 978-1-315-77660-6 (ebk)

Typeset in Bembo
by Apex CoVantage, LLC

Please be aware that some of the topics covered in this book may be considered challenging and sensitive, in order to engage students and stimulate debate. Teachers should use their best judgement regarding appropriateness when planning lessons, taking into account their own students' beliefs, levels of maturity, and personal experiences.

Printed and bound in the United States of America by Publishers Graphics, LLC on sustainably sourced paper.

Contents

Meet the Authors

Victor J. Moeller has taught College Rhetoric, English and American literature, and Philosophy in public and private high schools and colleges. As an inservice field instructor of the Chicago Great Books Foundation for 14 years, he conducted teacher training courses in 36 states and became Minnesota Area Director of professional development. Since 2007, he has been Reader for the AP English Literature and Language Exam and consultant for the College Board of Evanston, IL. All of Moeller's textbooks define, illustrate and demonstrate how to implement the Socratic method of teaching and learning in the humanities. Moeller has Master's degrees in English, Education, and Philosophy. He currently teaches at McHenry County College, Crystal Lake, IL and Elgin Community College, Elgin, IL.

Marc V. Moeller has taught courses in high schools and middle schools ranging from AP English, Composition, and English literature to English as a second language. He has a Master's degree in education from National Louis University of Chicago. He readily admits that the greatest impacton his teaching career has been Victor Moeller, his father and mentor. Marc Moeller currently teaches English at Prairie Middle School in Barrington, Illinois, and may be reached by **email at victormoeller.com**.

Preface

- "Students enter school as question marks and graduate as periods."
  Neil Postman
- "Reading is the only art form in which the audience plays the score; no other art requires the audience to be a performer."
  Kurt Vonnegut
- "When we read too fast or too slow, we understand nothing."
  Blaise Pascal
- "Reading and without discussion is like cooking without eating."
  Tom Romano
- "If you do not read, you will know only what you think."
  John Cheever
- "Authentic learning begins when teachers challenge students with real questions–problems about meaning that demand solutions."
  Victor Moeller
- "In training a child the activity of thought, above all things we must beware of 'inert ideas'—that is, ideas that are merely received into the mind without being utilized, or tested, or thrown into fresh combinations. Education with inert ideas is not only useless it is above all things, harmful."
  Alfred North Whitehead
- "Good discussion calls for the best teachers and I am convinced furthermore that it accomplishes more than any other form of teaching."
  Jacques Barzan
- "For Socrates, teaching was not merely asking a series of questions. . . . He wanted to make every pupil realize that truth was in the pupil's own power to find, if he searched long enough and hard enough, refusing all 'authoritative statements' and judged every solution by reason alone. This system is the most difficult, the least common, and yet the most thorough way to teach."
  Gilbert Highet

- "The ideal Socratic seminar occurs when the teacher is able to resort only to questions—when there is no declarative, teacher-talk, but only the asking of questions . . . The more the seminar is an experience of active learning for the students, the sooner they will become active learners in their reading of texts for future seminars and the sooner they will be able to engage in learning by themselves without the help of teachers, which is the ultimate goal of all teaching."

  Mortimer Adler

- "Good schools promote the habit of respectful skepticism . . . Asking questions captures our minds more readily than memorizing somebody else's answers to yet somebody else's questions."

  Theodore Sizer

- "What students most need to learn in schools is how to learn. The emphasis must be on the *how* of learning rather than the *what*."

  Neil Postman

Dear Colleague,

If you agree with most or at least some of the above statements, you have found a kindred spirit. As I shake your hand and get a chair for you, let me explain briefly how this book will help you become a better teacher. Everything in this text is based on the assumption that students not teachers, are the primary agents in learning. The corollary is that authentic learning is active learning. The consequence is that students become responsible for their own learning.

I have been writing this book in my imagination for the last 10 years. It describes, illustrates, and explains how to engage in the Socratic method of discussion and learning. However, just as no book on tennis can make you a good tennis player so neither can a book on active learning make you a proficient teacher. Nevertheless, with sustained effort, practice, experimentation, guidance, and willingness to learn from your mistakes, and use of video film, you can learn how to become an active learner along with your students. Better yet, take a Basic Leader Training Course from the Great Books Foundation or the National Paideia Center Training Program of NC. Check their web sites for course listings. See also online teacher conferences for collaborators: **www.englishcompanion.ning.com**

Sincerely,
Marc Moeller

Acknowledgments

"We are as pygmies standing on the shoulders of giants."

St. Bernard of Clairvaux

I must give credit where it is due. Much of what I know about the **Socratic method** of teaching, I learned from my teacher Mortimer Adler during my 14 years at the Great Books Foundation. While most of the ideas that I present here are my own that I have developed and refined over my last 10 years in the classroom, the basic ideas are found in Adler's writings (see References).

Copyright Notifications

PART

I

The Socratic Method

CHAPTER

1 Two Models of Teaching

If Good Teaching is a Dialogue, Why Does the Monologue Continue to Dominate?

Robert Benchley once remarked that: "There are two kinds of people—those who classify things and those who don't." Since I belong to the first group, I tend to classify teachers according to those who still employ the lecture model of learning and those who daily engage their students in active learning. I do so not only because most of my former teachers assumed that they were the most important part of the learning process but also because the lecture method continues to dominate in too many classrooms even today. In contrast, the Socratic teacher knows that the student is the most important part of the learning process.

Take my high school American literature teacher, Marc Prosser. He began most lessons by stating the objective: "By the end of this class you will be able to identify the characteristics of the 'code hero' in Hemingway"—and then, anticipating the so-what looks on our faces, explained the relevance or importance of this knowledge: "Hemingway's concept of the 'code hero' will give you standards by which to judge your own ideas of heroism." The class proceeded as a lecture. Mr. Prosser knew what a code hero was and he was going to tell us, tell us that he told us, and then ask us to tell him what he had told us. Our job as students was to "pay attention," that is, to be receptive and passive and to take careful, detailed notes. We were not to interrupt his lecture with comments; however, we were allowed to ask questions for elementary clarification. For example, "What do you mean by pragmatic?" or "Who is James L. Roberts?" or "Why do you call this stuff 'literary criticism'?" His authority was supreme, his answers all we needed to know on those subjects. After all, he had a Master's degree.

His lessons concluded with an objective test. "I am the tester, and you are the testees," he would say, and never would we break from those roles.

However, "to be fair"—another of his pet phrases—he "entertained" questions before the test. If we had none, Mr. Prosser judged his lesson a success. In the end, we were to trust that Mr. Prosser knew best even when we did not know what he was talking about. "Someday you will understand, and all will be clear," he would reassure us.

What I eventually came to understand, thanks to my college contemporary literature professor, Kenelm Basil, was that there was a better way to teach. Mr. Basil was a Socratic teacher if ever there was one. He began each lesson not by telling us what we were going to learn (he was not certain that we would learn anything although that was, of course, his fondest hope) but by posing a major problem about the meaning of the day's assigned text (a work of art whether written, created, or performed). He began always with a basic question of interpretation, wrote it on the board, and then asked each of us to write down our own initial answers on scrap paper. For example, "According to Vonnegut's story, 'Harrison Bergeron,' is the desire to excel as strong as the tendency to be mediocre?" Because he kept his own opinions to himself—he was not a participant but a leader—and he asked only follow-up questions on our comments, Mr. Basil convinced us over time that he really did not have a single correct answer in mind. Indeed, the class soon realized that more than one correct answer was possible because evidence from the story supported differing views. In short, our teacher began the discussion with a real question, the answer to which he himself was uncertain or even had no answer at all.

As students, we had to be active: clarifying our answers, testing others' answers for supporting evidence, resolving conflicting answers with evidence, and listening for more opinions. Learning in Mr. Basil's classroom was not about receiving ideas but about wrestling with them. The test of truth was reason and evidence, not teacher authority. The lesson concluded with a resolution activity since, after all, questions are quests for answers. We were asked to review our original responses and then to write a paragraph or a brief essay stating our comprehensive answer to the basic question. Most importantly, Mr. Basil strove not for group consensus or truth by vote, but rather for individual understandings: "Given the answers that you have just heard in discussion, what now is *your* solution?"

Liberation at last! I no longer had to sit dutifully silent while someone told me what I could just as easily have read for myself, found in a library, or researched on the Internet. I no longer had to parrot the teacher's interpretations. More important, Mr. Basil challenged me to think independently and to become responsible for my own ideas. The responsibility for learning had been placed in my hands and along with it, the joy and personal satisfaction of arriving at my own insights. I had learned to live with doubt and to uncover questions that answers hide. In short, I had learned how to learn.

Do not misunderstand. Most so-called Socratic teachers do not conduct discussions the way Mr. Basil did. Many have not mastered the art of fostering reflective, independent thinking. Such teachers confuse the right to express an opinion with the notion that any opinion can be right. Toleration of any and all ideas becomes the goal, and brain storming—that pathetic analogy—gets enthroned as the method. As one mindless person put it, "Don't we all know that everything is relative and that there are no absolutes?" Except, of course, his opinion.

Others, the pseudo-Socratic teachers, offer little more than a disguised lecture. These teachers pretend to conduct open discussions but have specific answers in mind. They tip their hands in several ways: by asking leading questions ("How can you honestly think Vonnegut would agree with you?"), by allowing opinions that they agree with go unchallenged or unsubstantiated, by developing a single line of argument on but one side of an issue, by injecting their own opinion into the discussion ("I believe that you have all overlooked important information on page six"), by commenting on student answers ("That's very good, James. I'm so proud of you" or, "Maria, I think you had better reconsider your answer. You are missing something"), and finally, by attempting to arrive at group consensus ("I would like to see a show of hands. How many think the desire to excel is as strong as the tendency to be mediocre?"). If what I have said about these would-be Socratic teachers is not true, how else are we to explain these examples of common student and teacher behaviors?

Teacher: Whenever I try to have a discussion, my students clam up. Only one or two contribute. They just don't get the point. I *have* to tell them.

Student: My answer is correct, isn't it Mrs. Jones?

Teacher: Discussion is a waste of time. I have to cover the curriculum.

Student: But Mrs. Jones, what *is* the right answer?

Teacher: My students' test scores have to improve. I don't have time for the luxury of endless discussions. I have 130 students. Get real.

Student: Why do you keep asking questions when you know the answers?

Teacher: Students don't know how to ask good questions and anyway, discussions are just too messy.

Student: Just let me alone and give me my C. I don't mess up your class.

Teacher: My students cannot be trusted to think for themselves. They keep coming up with silly answers.

But isn't that just the point? The lecturing teacher fails to understand that wrong answers are a necessary part of the learning process when real thinking takes place. In contrast, the authentic Socratic teacher recognizes and accepts false turns and "silly" answers as inevitable when students have the freedom to be wrong—*and* right. After all, thinking *is* difficult and students resist it like the plague. Any teacher will recognize immediately the common cop-outs: "I don't know," or "Why did you call on me?" or "I wasn't doing anything," or "Who cares?" or "What difference does it make?" and "Ask somebody else." In the end, if thinking were easy, there would be more of it.

The fundamental difference between Mr. Prosser and Mr. Basil comes down to who is finally responsible for learning. Mr. Prosser's approach implies that the teacher is, while Mr. Basil's suggests that students should be. Can anyone convince students they are responsible for their own learning other than students themselves? And is it not usually through discussion, dialogue, and problem solving—not through lecture—that students come to realize what they *have* and *have not* learned?

Not long ago, I heard James Howard of the Council for Basic Education state on National Public Radio say: "Education is what you have left after you have forgotten everything you learned in school." I wonder what Mr. Prosser would make of that statement. I know what Mr. Basil would do with it.

Two Models of Teaching and Learning

Didactic Passive Learning (Master–disciple)	Socratic Active Learning (Engaged inquiry)
1. Teacher centered: based on the assumption that the teacher is the primary agent in learning.	1. Problem centered: based on the assumption that the student is the primary agent in learning.
2. Teacher's role: to impart the results of experience, personal study, and reflection.	2. Teacher's role: to uncover the question that the answer hides. To be a co-learner.
3. Primarily deductive: the usual methods are lecture, story telling, use of analogy, and aphorism.	3. Primarily inductive: the usual methods are discussion, dialogue, and problem solving.
4. Test of truth: authority and experience.	4. Test of truth: reason and evidence.
5. Learning is the reception of ideas.	5. Learning is a conflict of ideas: a thesis, antithesis, and a synthesis that results in new knowledge (Hegel).
6. Student's role: to be passive, open, receptive, trusting, and unquestioning.	6. Student's role: to be active, questioning, critical, and discriminating—learning to trust one's own judgment (independent thinking).
7. Evaluation is factual recall of data—commonly in the form of objective tests (right and wrong answers).	7. Evaluation is application of understanding interpretation of data—commonly in an essay, speech, journal, or a review.
8. Ultimate goal: wisdom viewed as the internalization of truths and beliefs.	8. Ultimate goal: wisdom viewed as an informed ignorance (knowing what one does not know—the Socratic paradox).

While the article illustrates the importance of the Socratic method for active learning, the didactic model still has *a necessary but ancillary role* since teachers must sometimes provide organized information not accessible in other ways. A comparison–contrast outline of two generic lesson plans reveals important differences.

Lesson Plan Models

Didactic Infusion	Socratic Discovery
1. Focus: motivator.	1. Focus: attention grabber.
2. Objective: what students will be able to do by end of the lesson.	2. Objective: to solve problems. What students learn cannot be stated in advance.
3. Purpose: why lesson is important, useful, and relevant.	3. Purpose: to increase understanding and enjoyment of the group task by developing the habit of independent, critical, and reflective thinking.
4. Input: new information or activities.	4. Input: basic questions of interpretation and the co-leader's related, prepared follow-up questions of interpretation.
5. Modeling: verbal or physical example of acceptable finished product or process.	5. Modeling: the co-leaders follow the Four Rules of Socratic Discussion.
6. Checking: determine if students have the information needed to complete the task.	6. Checking: co-leaders ask spontaneous follow-up question for clarification, substantiation, more opinion, consistency, implication, relevance, and resolution.
7. Guided practice: task done independently in small groups with teacher help.	7. Guided practice: students learn how to rely on their own judgment about which answers are good, better, or best, and to distinguish the false from the true.
8. Closure: summary of what should have been learned. Objective is restated.	8. Closure: a written or oral resolution to problem(s) of interpretation.

CHAPTER

2 What is the Socratic Method of Teaching and Learning?

"The role of the teacher is to uncover the question that the answer hides."
James Baldwin

Let us begin at the source. Like so many students before him and even those today, Socrates' student Meno is exasperated by his teacher's refusal to "just tell him" what to do, what the truth is, and in their dialogue, whether or not virtue can be taught. Meno is astounded when Socrates openly admits that not only does he not know whether virtue can be taught but also that he does not even know what virtue is. "What!?" Meno asks: "Is this the report we are to take home about you?" In characteristic manner, Socrates challenges his student to rephrase the question, to reflect on it, and to arrive at his own answers. In so doing, Socrates helps Meno to wrestle with the implications of the problem that he has posed for their discussion. Indeed, Socrates makes a point of asserting his own ignorance: "All I can say is that I have often looked to see if there are any [teachers of virtue], and in spite of all my efforts, I cannot find them. . . . I do not know what virtue is and, not only that, you may say also, that to the best of my belief, I have never yet met anyone who did know" (Rouse 1995: 29). Meno leaves, confounded that his teacher, his master and guide refuses to confirm what Meno believes he already knows.

Nevertheless, when Socrates' reputation for wisdom continues to grow, another impetuous student, Chaerephon, goes to the oracle of Delphi to ask if anyone is wiser than Socrates. The priestess of Apollo, Pythia, replies that no one is. When Socrates hears the answer, he is genuinely puzzled: "I have no wisdom, small or great. What can she mean when she says that I am the wisest of men?" (Rouse 1995: 426). But why does Socrates take the oracle's word at face value? Could the god also have meant that no one was wiser than Socrates because wisdom is not to be found among men? Socrates is even more explicit about his ignorance in the defense of his life at his trial, *The Apology*. After questioning another who claimed to be wise, Socrates concludes, "I am better off than he is—for he knows nothing, and thinks that he knows; I neither know nor think that I know. In this latter particular, then, I seem to have the slight advantage over him" (327). What we have here is the great paradox of learning: you must first know what you want to know or recognize what you do not know. Is this confusing? Only at first. What Socrates suggests is that the first step to learning is knowing how to ask an honest question—one that you have no answer to or one that you have several answers to but none of which satisfy. In short, unless you have questions, you cannot learn. As learning begins, the more you know, the more you realize that you do not know. Such is the Socratic paradox.

But what about the Socratic method? The phrase is as elusive as a greased pig. What does this method mean to the teacher in the trenches? For some, unfortunately, it means no more than asking a lot of questions—rapidly and indiscriminately. For others, it means conducting an interview. And for still others it means cross-examination. A few even seem to believe that there is something mystical about the Socratic method—that some teachers are born with it or that there really is no common method at all that other teachers can acquire. Nevertheless, all of these notions miss the mark because they fail to capture the Socratic concept of teaching *and* do not recognize that the Socratic method can be explained, applied, and evaluated. Furthermore, there is no "official" Socratic method since even today there is no consensus about Socrates' method as recorded in the dialogues of his most brilliant student, Plato. Nevertheless, based on my career with the Great Books Foundation and my mentor Mortimer Adler, as well as my extensive experience in the classroom, I am confident enough to assert my own conception of a Socratic method in the following exposition.

What is the Socratic method? It is an exercise in "reflective thinking" that, according to John Dewey (1997) has two elements: *doubt*—a problem about meaning which initiates it—and *an act of searching* for a solution(s) to solve that problem.

How is it done? It is conducted mainly by asking *prepared questions* (the problems which are the focus of discussion) and *spontaneous follow-up questions* that develop the ideas being considered with a view to achieving resolution.

Why is it done this way? It is done this way to achieve the goal or purpose of this kind of engaged learning: to increase the groups' *and* the co-leaders' understanding (comprehension) of the text under discussion. *As a result*, there will be also an increase in enjoyment—that is, the satisfaction of discovering one's own answers and finding new meaning(s) in the selection.

Co-leaders are student pairs, teacher pairs, or teacher–student pairs who have been trained in the following method of discussion. But why do you need co-leaders? For several reasons: (1) Thinking continuously, keeping track of ideas, and deciding which answers to develop with spontaneous follow-up questions requires a high degree of concentration. Two leaders provide more mental power and ordinarily do a better job than a single leader; (2) Two leaders provide a good model of teamwork by working together just as the participants are expected to work together in solving the problem. Co-leaders also instill in the group a belief that they can learn from each other, and a willingness to assume a share of responsibility for the outcome of the discussion. Also, a pair of co-leaders are less likely to be viewed as "authority" figures; (3) To follow up ideas and, at the same time, to observe and to recognize those who want to speak and to invite the reluctant to participate, two sets of eyes and ears are needed; Finally, (4) co-leaders need one another to prepare properly for discussion. A co-leader ought never to say to his or her partner, "It is your question, sink or swim with it." On the contrary, it must be *our* previously agreed-upon prepared questions that are the focus of discussion; it must also be *our* spontaneous follow-up questions that develop and provide the structure needed for authentic learning to happen in discussion.

In sum, the Socratic method begins with a *problem* (a prepared interpretive question), continues as a *process* of asking spontaneous follow-up questions, and results in a *product*—a resolution, increased understanding, and enjoyment of the text.

The Four Rules of Socratic Discussion

1. **First, no one may participate who has not read the selection before discussion.** The ticket of admission is that everyone has read the selection carefully. For this reason, before discussion the leader(s) begins with a plot-check quiz—that is, a list of factual questions that anyone can readily answer if he or she has done the reading. Those who have not done the reading are limited to the role of spectators. For less-able readers, this rule can be obviated on occasion by making the first reading an oral one in class. Another helpful technique is to conduct textual analysis, at times, when a group is not well prepared or has read the text only once.
2. **Second, participants must support answers with textual evidence.** Without evidence, discussion soon becomes a matter of sheer conjecture wherein one idea begins to sounds as good as another. Without evidence participants have no way of deciding which answers are better than others and which are wrong. Evidence turns mere opinion into interpretation. After all, there are right and wrong answers in discussion just as some interpretations are better than others.

3. **Third, participants may not introduce outside authorities but discuss only the assigned readings.** This rule also ensures that everyone has equal access to the same information upon which everyone has to base his or her answers. The logical starting point for discussion is the reading itself. In their *Theory of Literature*, Warren and Wellek get to the heart of the matter:

   > The natural sensible starting point for work in literary scholarship is interpretation and analysis of the works of literature themselves. After all, only the works themselves justify all our interest in the life of an author, in his social environment, and the whole process of literature. But curiously enough, literary history has been so preoccupied with the setting of a work of literature that its attempts at analysis of the works themselves have been slight in comparison with the enormous efforts expended on the study of their background.

   Furthermore, students learn to become responsible for their own ideas when they do not try to justify them by appealing to an authority—another book or another person. They must learn to rely on their own judgment about the meaning of the text (a work of art whether written, created, or performed).
4. **Most importantly, the co-leaders may ask only questions.** The moment the co-leaders begin making statements during discussion, the atmosphere changes from independent thinking and mutual inquiry to attempts to please the leaders. Even worse, the vociferous can quickly turn discussion into an argument or debate. Furthermore, no matter how well intentioned, leaders' comments hinder participants' opportunity to think independently and freely. And finally, the co-leader's primary role to develop and relate ideas becomes practically impossible when one or both become participants.

CHAPTER

3 Lesson Plan 1

Active and Close Reading

1. **Focus:**	How important is reading in your life? Do you enjoy reading? If so, why so? If not, why not? (Brief discussion or journal.)
2. **Objective:**	To develop and to apply the techniques of Active and Close Reading.
3. **Purpose:**	○ To increase our mutual understanding (comprehension) and, as a result, our enjoyment of reading. ○ To develop the habit of independent and critical thinking.
4. **Input:**	Oral reading: "Active and Close Reading."
5. **Modeling, checking, and guided practice:**	As you go over the handout, answer any student questions or emphasize any ideas as needed. *Model* your notations on the poem by Robert Frost after you have asked the students to make their own notations. *Compare notations*: what the students thought was important, what they didn't understand, what they liked or disliked, agreed or disagreed with, whatever they think related (connections). *Read silently the first page* of "Gaston" by William Saroyan in preparation for the following Lessons (2–5). Ask students for examples of their notations on page 1 of the reading.
6. **Closure:**	*Assignment*: To be able to understand the illustrations used in the next four lessons, please read twice the short story by William Saroyan, "Gaston." On the first reading, make notations on what is important, what you don't understand, what you like or dislike, agree or disagree with, and whatever you find related. On the second reading, convert some of your notations into at least eight questions. Include a page reference for each.

Active and Close Reading

"I read slower than I write."

John Updike

"Reading is the only art form in which the audience plays the score; no other art requires the audience to be a performer."

Kurt Vonnegut

"When we read too fast or too slow, we understand nothing."

Blaise Pascal

"The person who does not spend as much time in actively and definitely thinking about what he has read as he has spent in reading, is simply insulting the author."

M. Arnold

A first step for participating in the Seminar is reading the selection. Far too many students read neither actively nor closely—not only because they have not learned how to discriminate among the various purposes of different kinds of reading but also because they have not been taught how to read actively. Here is a method that I have found productive if employed continually by teacher and student.

The phrase "active and close reading" suggests immediately two ideas. First, some books and stories deserve to be read closely, slowly, and actively—not only because we would miss many of their implied meanings but also because we must learn to recognize meanings other than our own in what we peruse. Second, there are times when how fast we read or how much we read is of no importance. What *is* important is that we learn **to reflect** on what we read and learn how to carry on a conversation with the author. We converse with an author when we question always the text.

The purpose of active and close reading is to learn to read interpretively—to pay attention not merely to *what* an author says but to *why* he says it in the *way* that he does. In short, the purpose in reading is not merely trying to recall what happens in a story, for example, but to think about why things happen as they do. With nonfiction, active readers take particular note of an author's choice of words (diction), use of sentence structure (syntax), and his or her organization of ideas.

Some books and stories, like those that we will be reading, can be **interpreted in several ways.** And no individual, adult or child, teacher or student, ever thinks of *all* of the possible interpretations in a given selection. As a result, no one can tell you what is *the* correct interpretation of a story, poem, or play—not even, believe it or not, the author! However, this does *not* mean that all interpretations are equally good or correct. On the contrary, some interpretations are better than others and some are wrong. How can this be so? The answer is that some interpretations have more evidence to support them, which makes them more plausible. Other interpretations are more comprehensive—that is, they explain more of a text than does another view. Still other interpretations are wrong: either there is no evidence to support them or the evidence offered is contradicted by some other statement of the author. But what about the author? Why doesn't he or she have the last word about what was "really meant"?

Thomas Mann, in the extraordinary afterword of his novel, "The Making of *The Magic Mountain*" (page 725) says:

> I consider it a mistake to think that the author himself is the best judge of his work. He may be that while he is still at work on it and living in it. But once done, it tends to be something he has got rid of, something foreign to him; others, as time goes on, will know more and better about it than he. *They can often remind him of things in it he has forgotten or indeed never quite knew.*

Just as no one can tell you what is *the* correct interpretation nor what your interpretation must be, so also no one can tell you **what details** in your reading are important. Meaning can begin anywhere—even with what someone else might regard an insignificant detail. Whatever furnishes you with clues for arriving at your own interpretation, that is what is important. In short, what is important varies from reader to reader.

In addition, to interpret a work for yourself does *not* require that you first read about the author's life, or about the times in which the author lived, nor review general introductory or background statements. Instead, readers can begin by noting their responses to a story and then trying to convert as many of them as possible into questions. But to engage in this process fruitfully, readers must learn to respect their own responses—that is, to take seriously their thoughts and feelings about a book.

Forming good questions whose answers can yield a great deal of meaning about a story requires at least **two readings**. Roland Barthes, the eminent French literary critic, maintains that, "He who reads a story only once is condemned to read the same story his whole life" (1975). On the **first reading**, the readers' main interest should be to note their responses in writing—that is, to make notations. Tom Romano, a New York high school English teacher, says that: "Reading without writing [here, notations] is like cooking without eating." During the **second reading**, readers note new responses and pay special attention to those notations that they can convert into questions.

Unless readers learn to put their responses into writing by making notations as they read, they will have few questions—or, if there are any questions at all, they will be so general that they could be asked of any story. Such generic questions yield little new knowledge and yet without questions, no one can increase his understanding of the material. The first step to learning then is, paradoxically, knowing what you want to know—that is, asking real questions.

As American philosopher and educator Mortimer Adler (1940) explains in his classic essay on "How to Mark a Book," a notation is any response to the text that a reader puts into writing. Notations take various forms: underlining what is important, circling key words, drawing lines to make connections between similar parts, comments, personal, emotional reactions, reminders, and even nascent questions. As John Ruskin so aptly remarked, "No book is worth anything which is not worth much; nor is it serviceable until it has been read and reread, and loved, and loved again, and marked." Serviceable is the key word.

Experienced readers have found that whenever they mark up a text, they usually refer to one or more of **four sources** for formulating questions:

1. **Whatever they think is important** (for whatever reason).
2. **Whatever they don't understand.** Not understanding something is more than circling unfamiliar vocabulary (although it includes this). It also means making notations about a character's motivation, for example, or why the story begins or ends as it does, or what the author means by a certain statement or includes a certain scene, and so on.
3. **Whatever they like or dislike, agree or disagree with.** In other words, active readers are also careful to note their emotional responses. For Louise Rosenblatt (1962, Part II), this step is crucial—what the reader brings to the text.
4. **Whatever they think is related**—one part of the text to another. A chief concern of the second reading is looking for connections or patterns among various parts of the reading. For example:
   (a) The repetition of the same word or phrase.
   (b) The reoccurrence of similar actions.
   (c) Contrasting words or actions.
   (d) The place of something in the text (organization).

As with so many things, whatever we get out of an enterprise is proportionate to the effort we put into it. So too with reading. Unless we learn how to become thoughtful, active, and close readers, we will continue to miss many of the implications of what we read and, as a result, lose the pleasure of increasing our understanding of the text.

Directions: Mark up the poem below by questioning what you think is important, circling key words, drawing lines to make connections, comments, and personal emotional reactions.

The Road Not Taken

Robert Frost

Two roads diverged in a yellow wood,
And sorry I could not travel both
And be one traveler, long I stood
And looked down one as far as I could
To where it bent in the undergrowth;

Then took the other, just as fair,
And having perhaps the better claim,
Because it was grassy and wanted wear;
Though as for the passing there
Had worn them really about the same,

And both that morning equally lay
In leaves no step had trodden black.
Oh, I kept the first for another day!
Yet knowing how way leads on to way,
I doubted if I should ever come back.

I shall be telling this with a sigh
Somewhere ages and ages hence:
Two roads diverged in a yellow wood, and I—
I took the one less traveled by,
And that has made all the difference.

First Reading: Notations

1. Whatever you think important:
   The narrator really would like to have taken both roads (line 3).
   The narrator admits the two roads were really about the same (10).
   The narrator is talking about a major decision (16).

2. Whatever you don't understand.
   Why isn't the title about the road less traveled?
   Why will the speaker be telling about his decision with a sigh?

3. Whatever you like or dislike, agree or disagree with.
   Whenever I make an important decision, I too sometimes wonder what would have happened if I had chosen differently.

4. Whatever you think is related:
   (a) The repetition of the same word or phrase.
       First and eighteenth line.
   (b) The reoccurrence of similar actions.
       Choosing to look back on a previous choice.
   (c) Contrasting words or actions.
       Speaking about a decision and making that decision.
   (d) The place of something in the text (organization).
       Which word(s) of the last line need(s) emphasis?

Second Reading: Notations Converted into Questions

1. Why isn't the title of the poem "The Road Less Traveled"?
2. Why is the choice of the less traveled road made on a fall morning? (lines 1, 11)
3. Why would the narrator like to have taken both roads? (2, 13)
4. Why does the narrator say that one road had "perhaps" the better claim? (7)
5. Why does the narrator admit the two roads were really much the same? (10)
6. Why is there an exclamation point at the end of line 13?
7. Does the narrator sigh out of satisfaction or regret? (16)
8. Will the narrator be telling of his choice to others or only to himself? (16)
9. Why does the narrator think he will be speaking of his decision in the distant future? (17)

On Reading Nonfiction

But what about nonfiction? Do these active reading techniques for fiction apply equally to non-fiction? Yes and no. The same basic techniques of making notations, writing questions, and so on apply also to nonfiction, which is commonly defined as "all forms of prose that purport to be factual" and use exposition, argumentation, and fictions only to illustrate. However, with factual prose, particular attention must be given to: (1) identifying the author's thesis (what) and purpose (why); (2) his audience (who); (3) his style (how) of writing—diction, syntax, vocabulary, and use of examples; (4) the structure and organization of ideas; (5) the relationships among the principal sections of the text; and (6) above all, his tone or attitude toward his topic must be determined. As the College Board people continually remind us: "To miss the tone is to miss the meaning." In Part III, you will find several good examples of how these techniques have been applied to nonfiction (Martin Luther King, etc.).

Textual Analysis

Textual analysis is a detailed examination of a particular passage in which you try to determine the author's meaning line by line and sometimes word by word. This technique is a good way to get into a reading when the group has not read well enough to participate in an interpretive discussion. In addition to being a remedial device, when co-leaders use textual analysis, they model what should be happening during the first and second readings. Finally, textual analysis is also effective even when the group is doing well in discussion; in this situation, textual analysis builds on ideas already expressed to draw out more meaning from specific passages that help to resolve the basic question. Textual analysis involves four steps in this order:

1. **Select a passage** that you want to examine closely and have a group participant read it aloud. Oral reading is not only an important aid to understanding but also an indicator of a student's level of comprehension of what he or she is reading.
2. **Identify the speaker of the passage,** the narrator. It may be the author speaking directly to you, a fictional narrator, an anonymous narrator, or a character speaking to another character.
3. **Identify the context of the passage.** If you have chosen a passage other than the beginning or the conclusion of the story, try to get a rough idea of where you are in the selection. In short, ask questions about what happened just prior to the passage and what happened just after it.

4. **Review the passage line by line and even key words.** This step is the heart of textual analysis and the most important. Go over the difficult passage, line by line, freely asking questions of fact or of interpretation about the meaning of words, phrases, and sentences about which you are uncertain of the answer. Freely turn to other sections of the reading that you think are related to the passage being explored. After you have reviewed the entire passage, return to your basic question by restating or rephrasing it and then continue the discussion.

Reading Assignment

To be able to understand the examples used in the following pages of exposition, please read twice the short story by **William Saroyan, "Gaston."** On the first reading, make notations on what is important, what you don't understand, what you like or dislike, agree or disagree with, and whatever you find related one part of the story to the other. On the second reading, convert some of your notations into questions.

Gaston

William Saroyan

They were to eat peaches, as planned, after her nap, and now she sat across from the man who would have been a total stranger except that he was in fact her father. They had been together again (although she couldn't quite remember when they had been together before) for almost a hundred years now, or was it only since day before yesterday? Anyhow, they were together again, and he was kind of funny. First, he had the biggest mustache she had ever seen on anybody, although to her it was not a mustache at all; it was a lot of red and brown hair under his nose and around the ends of his mouth. Second, he wore a blue-and-white striped jersey instead of a shirt and tie, and no coat. His arms were covered with the same hair, only it was a little lighter and thinner. He wore blue slacks, but no shoes and socks, He was barefoot, and so was she, of course.

He was at home. She was with him in his home in Paris, if you could call it a home. He was very old, especially for a young man: thirty-six, he had told her; and she was six, just up from sleep on a very hot afternoon in August.

That morning, on a little walk in the neighborhood, she had seen peaches in a box outside a small store and she had stopped to look at them, so he had bought a kilo. Now, the peaches were on a large plate on the card table at which they sat. There were seven of them, but one of them was flawed. It looked as good as others, almost the size of a tennis ball, nice red fading to light green, but where the stem had been there was now a break that went straight down into the heart of the seed. He placed the biggest and best-looking peach on the small plate in front of the girl, and then took the flawed peach and began to remove the skin. When he had half the skin off the peach he ate that side, neither of them talking, both of them just being there, and not being excited or anything: no plans, that is. The man held the half-eaten peach in his fingers and looked down into the cavity, into the open seed. The girl looked too.

While they were looking, two feelers poked out from the cavity. They were attached to a kind of brown knob-head, which followed the feelers, and then two large legs took a strong grip on the edge of the cavity and hoisted some of the rest of whatever it was out of the seed, and stopped there a moment, as if to look around. The man studied the seed dweller, and so, of course, did the girl. The creature paused only a fraction of a second, and then continued to come out of the seed, to walk down the eaten side of the peach to wherever it was going.

The girl had never seen anything like it: a whole big thing made out of brown color, a knob-head, feelers, and a great many legs. It was very active too. Almost businesslike, you might say. The man placed the peach back on the plate. The creature moved off the peach onto the surface of the white plate. There it came to a thoughtful stop.

"Who is it?" the girl said.

"Gaston."

"Where does he live?"

"Well, he used to live in this peach seed, but now that the peach has been harvested and sold, and I have eaten half of it, it looks as if he's out of house and home."

"Aren't you going to squash him?"

"No, of course not, why should I?"

"He is a bug. He is ugh."

"Not at all. He is Gaston the grand boulevardier."

"Everybody hollers when a bug comes out of an apple, but you don't holler or anything."

"Of course not. How should we like if somebody hollered every time we came out of our house?"

"Why would they?"

"Precisely. So why should we holler at Gaston?"

"He is not the same as us."

"Well, not exactly, but he's the same as a lot of other occupants of peach seeds. Now, the poor fellow hasn't got a home, and there he is with all that pure design and handsome form, and nowhere to go."

"Handsome?"

"Gaston is just about the handsomest of his kind I've ever seen."

"What's he saying?"

"Well, he's a little confused. Now, inside that house of his he had everything in order. Bed here, porch there, and so forth."

"Show me."

The man picked up the peach, leaving Gaston entirely alone on the white plate. He removed the peeling and ate the rest of the peach.

"Nobody else I know would do that," the girl said. "They'd throw it away."

"I can't imagine why. It's a perfectly good peach."

He opened the seed, placed the two sides not far from Gaston. The girl studied the open halves.

"Is that where he lives?"

"It's where he used to live. Gaston is out in the world and on his own now. You can see for yourself how comfortable he was in there. He had everything."

"Now what has he got?"

"Not very much, I'm afraid."

"What's he going to do?"

"What are we going to do?"

"Well, we're not going to squash him, that's one thing we're not going to do," the girl said.

"What are we going to do, then?"

"Put him back?"

"Oh, that house is finished."

"Well, he can't live in our house, can he?"

"Not happily."

"Can he live in our house at all?"

"Well, he could try, I suppose. Don't you want to eat a peach?"

"Only if it's a peach with somebody in the seed."

"Well, see if you can find a peach that has an opening at the top, because if you can, that'll be a peach in which you're likeliest to find somebody."

The girl examined each of the peaches on the big plate.

"They're all shut," she said.

"Well, eat one, then."

"No. I want the same kind that you ate, with somebody in the seed."

"Well, to tell you the truth, the peach I ate would be considered a bad peach, so of course stores don't like to sell them. I was sold that one by mistake, most likely. And so now Gaston is without a home, and we've got six perfect peaches to eat."

"I don't want a perfect peach. I want a peach with people."

"Well, I'll go out and see if I can find one."

"Where will I go?"

"You'll go with me, unless you'd rather stay. I'll only be five minutes."

"If the phone rings, what shall I say?"

"I don't think it'll ring, but if it does, say hello and see who it is."

"If it is my mother, what shall I say?"

"Tell her I've gone to get you a bad peach, and anything else you want to tell her."

"If she wants me to go back, what shall I say?"

"Say yes if you want to go back."

"Do you want me to?"

"Of course not, but the important thing is what you want, not what I want."

"Why is that the important thing?"

"Because I want you to be where you want to be."

"I want to be here."

"I'll be right back."

He put on socks and shoes, and a jacket, and went out. She watched Gaston trying to find out what to do next. Gaston wandered around the plate, but everything seemed wrong and he didn't know what to do or where to go.

The telephone rang and her mother said she was sending the chauffeur to pick her up because there was a little party for somebody's daughter who was also six, and then tomorrow they would fly back to New York.

"Let me speak to your father," she said.

"He's gone to get a peach."

"One peach?"

"One with people."

"You haven't been with your father two days and already you sound like him."

"There are peaches with people in them. I know. I saw one of them come out."

"A bug?"

"Not a bug. Gaston."

"Who?"

"Gaston the grand something."

"Somebody gets a peach with a bug in it, and throws it away, but not him. He makes up a lot of foolishness about it."

"It's not foolishness."

"All right, all right, don't get angry at me about a horrible peach bug of some kind."

"Gaston is right here, just outside his broken house, and I'm not angry at you."

"You'll have a lot of fun at the party."

"OK."

"We'll have fun flying back to New York, too."

"OK."

"Are you glad you saw your father?"

"Of course I am."

"Is he funny?"

"Yes."

"Is he crazy?"

"Yes. I mean, no. He just doesn't holler when he sees a bug crawling out of a peach seed or any-thing. He just looks at it carefully. But it is just a bug, isn't it, really?"

"That's all it is."

"And we have to squash it?"

"That's right. I can't wait to see you, darling. These two days have been like two years to me. Good-bye."

The girl watched Gaston on the plate, and she actually didn't like him. He was all ugh, as he had been in the first place. He didn't have a home anymore and he was wandering around on the white plate and he was silly and wrong and ridiculous and useless and all sorts of other things.

She cried a little, but only inside, because long ago she had decided she didn't like crying because if you ever started to cry it seemed as if there was so much to cry about you almost couldn't stop, and she didn't like that at all. The open halves of the peach seed were wrong, too. They were ugly or something. They weren't clean.

The man bought a kilo of peaches but found no flawed peaches among them, so he bought another kilo at another store, and this time his luck was better, and there were two that were flawed. He hurried back to his flat and let himself in. His daughter was in her room, in her best dress.

"My mother phoned," she said, "and she's sending the chauffeur for me because there's another birthday party."

"Another?"

"I mean, there's always a lot of them in New York."

"Will the chauffeur bring you back?"

"No. We're flying back to New York tomorrow."

"Oh."

"I liked being in your house."

"I liked having you here."

"Why do you live here?"

"This is my home."

"It's nice, but it's a lot different from our home."

"Yes, I suppose it is."

"It's kind of like Gaston's house."

"Where is Gaston?"

"I squashed him."

"Really? Why?"

"Everybody squashes bugs and worms."

"Oh. Well. I found you a peach."

"I don't want a peach anymore."

"OK."

He got her dressed, and he was packing her stuff when the chauffeur arrived. He went down the three flights of stairs with his daughter and the chauffeur, and in the street he was about to hug the girl when he decided he had better not. They shook hands instead, as if they were strangers. He watched the huge car drive off, and then he went around the corner where he took his coffee every morning, feeling a little, he thought, like Gaston on the white plate.

CHAPTER

4 Lesson Plan 2

Three Kinds of Questions

1. **Focus:**	*Overview*: Review several individual questions written on "Gaston" (previous assignment) by asking someone to answer each question orally. Does the answer turn us into the story? (If yes, it is factual OR interpretation). If we cannot disagree about the answer because it is given, it is factual ("What does it say?"). If we can disagree about the answer, it is interpretation ("What does it mean?"). If the answer *takes us outside the story* ("Is it true?"), it is evaluation.
2. **Objective:**	To identify and write questions of fact, interpretation, and evaluation.
3. **Purpose:**	○ To increase our mutual understanding (comprehension) and, as a result, our enjoyment of the reading. ○ To develop the habit of independent and critical thinking.
4. **Input:**	Explain and illustrate the three kinds of questions (see handout). Have students write on their handout the examples displayed on the board.
5. **Modeling, checking, and guided practice:**	Have students complete (in pairs or individually) Exercise 1 on Three Kinds of Questions. Review as a class the type of each question to check for understanding. To reinforce student understanding of the three kinds of questions, have them compose orally for review two or three sequences of related questions.
6. **Closure:**	Have students *combine and revise* (in pairs) the questions that they wrote individually on "Gaston." Hand in one sheet with two names of their ten best questions. Grade and return.

Three Kinds of Questions

"What does it say? What does it mean? Is it true?"

Mortimer Adler

When did you first realize the importance of the kinds of questions that you ask your students? Was it when you were puzzled about why some questions fell flat while others provoked immediate response? Was it when you suddenly realized your questions were not clear? Was it when you knew that you placed too much emphasis on factual or memory questions? Was it when you got into "bull sessions" as a consequence of emphasizing evaluative questions? Whatever the moment of insight, few teachers would deny the importance of writing and asking good questions. On the other hand, my experience has been that while teachers recognize that questioning is an art, they also too often are at a loss not only about how to write good discussion (interpretive) questions but also about how to sustain them in discussion.

Mortimer Adler, the eminent American philosopher and education reform leader, first formulated the three kinds of questions in 1948 in *A Guide for Leaders of Great Books Discussion Groups.* He asked: "(1) What does the author say? (2) What does he mean? (3) Is it true; does it have relevance to you here today? *Fact, Interpretation, Evaluation*—these are the three levels of questions." In 1956, Benjamin Bloom edited a *Taxonomy of Educational Objectives: Cognitive Domain*, which classified eight educational objectives that used examples of questions for each kind of thinking: knowledge (memory), comprehension, translation, interpretation, application, analysis, synthesis, and evaluation. Ten years later, Norris Sanders (1966) popularized Bloom's taxonomy for social studies teachers with useful illustrations in his *Classroom Questions: What Kinds?*

But do teachers need eight kinds of questions? Not in my experience. Too often have I been in workshops where teachers get into vigorous and pointless arguments about identifying types of questions. Bloom's and Sanders' work has its value for developing standardized tests, but for classroom discussion, their added distinctions are not needed since it becomes evident in discussion that translation, application, analysis, and synthesis can be put under the umbrella of interpretation. Knowledge or memory questions are factual and evaluation is about personal values and/or experience. In other words, classroom teachers do well enough, as do most of my colleagues, to recognize the vital difference between *the purpose* of each type of question: to check for recall (factual)? To check for understanding (interpretation)? Or to check for personal relevance and application (evaluation)? Here is how I explain and illustrate the three kinds of questions for my students.

Three Kinds of Questions

1. **Factual:** A factual question has but one correct answer. It asks the reader to recall something that the author said or to read a passage from the text where an answer can be found. Its answer depends more on memory than thinking.

   For example: *To what does the girl compare her father's home?*

   Note: Sometimes a factual question does require some thinking to answer correctly but it is still factual because only one answer is possible based on a careful reading of the text.

   For example: *Does the girl's mother have a low opinion of the girl's father?*

2. **Interpretation:** An interpretive question has more than one correct answer because a difference of opinion about meaning is possible. It asks the reader to explain *what the author means by what is said.* The answer depends more on thinking than on memory or recall.

   For example: *Is the girl's or the father's situation more like Gaston's?*

3. **Evaluation:** An evaluative question asks one to think about his or her own values or experiences. Such questions sometimes ask readers to consider how they would act in a situation similar to one a character in the story finds himself/herself in if they had a similar experience.

   For example (common experience): *How would you react if someone said you were crazy?*
   Or, for example (values): *Do you ridicule people who are different or unusual?*

   Note: The **test** for distinguishing between the three types of questions is to begin answering the question itself for a half minute. If you begin talking about the text, the question is factual or interpretive. If it has but one answer, it is factual; if it can be answered in more than one way, *if you have to explain your answer*, it is interpretive. If you begin to talk about your own experiences or values, if you go outside the text, it is evaluation.

Three Kinds of Questions

"GASTON" EXERCISE 1

Directions: First, answer each question briefly below or on your own paper. Second, at the left, in the margin, identify the type of each question: print FACT for factual, INT for interpretation, and EVAL for evaluation.

1. Why does the mother call the insect a bug but the father give it a name and personality?

2. Did the father buy more than one kilos of peaches for his daughter?

3. Would you rather live with the little girl's mother or her father?

4. Unlike the father, why does the mother persuade her daughter to stay with her?

5. Do we know why the girl's parents divorced?

6. Why does the girl finally decide to live with her mother rather than with her father?

7. Why does the mother ridicule the girl's father but the father say nothing bad about the girl's mother?

8. Why do some children of divorced parent have a hard time?

9. Why does the girl cry before she kills Gaston?

10. How did the father feel when his daughter returned to New York?

Writing Sequences of Related Questions

Here is another useful exercise that will give you further practice in testing your students' understanding of the differences between the three kinds of questions.

Directions: With your partner, write six interpretive questions on the reading with a page reference for each. Select your two best questions and then write a *related* question of fact and evaluation for each. Begin with a factual question. For example:

Factual: How does the father refer to the bug when it appears?

Interpretation: Unlike the mother, why does the father give the bug a name and a personality?

Evaluation: Would you have given the peach bug a name?

CHAPTER

5 Lesson Plan 3

Qualities of Good Discussion Questions

1. **Focus:**	Why do some questions elicit immediate response and even controversy while others fall flat or meet with apathy or indifference? (Brief discussion or journal topic.)
2. **Objective:**	To illustrate, identify, and write good discussion questions that are clear, specific, interpretive, answerable, and, most importantly, are *real questions*, questions that have the vital element of doubt about the answer.
3. **Purpose:**	○ To increase our mutual understanding (comprehension) and, as a result, our enjoyment of the reading. ○ To develop the habit of independent and critical thinking.
4. **Input:**	Review Six Qualities of Good Discussion Questions.
5. **Modeling, checking, and guided practice:**	Have students complete (in pairs or individually) **Exercise 2** on Qualities of Good Questions. Review as a class what is good about or lacking in each question. A good question will elicit at least two different, plausible answers based on the text.
6. **Closure:**	Review examples of good student questions that have been revised (previous assignment). Discuss briefly each question to elicit at least two different plausible answers. Ask for supporting textual evidence for each answer.

Qualities of Good Discussion Questions

"What are you asking me, Mr. M—?"

As a teacher or student, you must have been puzzled at times about why some questions in class fall flat while others evoke immediate response. While student inattention and unwillingness to think may explain some of the lack of response, we must also look at the quality of the questions that we ask. Some questions are so general or unclear that no one could hope for a reasonable response. In short, those questions that evoke next to no response may lack one of the important qualities of good prepared discussion questions, while those that generate ideas for discussion may have all the necessary qualities. Here is how I explain and illustrate the six characteristics of good discussion questions.

A Checklist of the Qualities of Good Discussion Questions

1. **Clear:** A clear question says what it means so that no one has to guess what the questioner has in mind. A question that is not clear is like asking someone to find something but not telling him/her what to look for. If the question has to be explained or if it cannot be rephrased, it is not clear. In short, the effort in discussion should be expended on trying to solve the problem, not in trying to figure out the question!
2. **Interpretive:** Since the primary aim of shared inquiry is to increase your own and the group's understanding of the reading, center on questions of interpretation. Factual questions do not generate discussion since they have but one correct answer and when questions of evaluation become the focus of discussion, it readily becomes a bull session.
3. **Specific:** A good discussion question must be specific, that is, tailor-made so that it could be asked only of one reading and not of another. This is not a matter of being picky or merely naming a character but a matter of being precise—that is, of pinpointing a problem about meaning.
4. **Doubt:** There must be doubt in the mind of the person who formulated the question for it to function in discussion. Without the vital element of doubt about the answer to the question, there can be no increase in understanding or insight. A question has the element of doubt **either** when the questioner can think of no answer at all **or**, as is the case more commonly, when the questioner can think of more than one answer but

none seems fully satisfactory. In this case, doubt is a matter of degree; it is not complete.

5. **Answerable** on the basis of the text alone. Avoid questions that go outside the text and ask a reader to offer a speculative answer, that is, one that cannot be supported one way or another from the text itself. Such questions are unsatisfactory because there is no way to judge which answers are plausible.
6. **Care or concern:** The co-leaders must ask questions that interest them, not what they think might interest someone else. This personal quality adds an intensity to discussion.

Qualities of Good Discussion Questions

"GASTON" EXERCISE 2

Directions: At the left of each question, on your own paper, mark GOOD if it has the qualities of a good discussion question. If the question lacks one of the needed qualities, mark it:

- NC if the question is NOT CLEAR.
- NS if the question is NOT SPECIFIC and could be asked of any story.
- LD for LACKS DOUBT because it cannot be answered in more than one way.
- NI for NOT INTERPRETIVE because it is factual or evaluation.
- NA if it is NOT ANSWERABLE on the basis of the text alone.

1. What is the main conflict in the story?

2. Will the girl ever see her father again?

3. Why does she act so weird?

4. To what does the girl compare her father's home?

5. Would you have killed the bug?

6. Does the author portray the girl as confused at times?

7. Why does the girl describe Gaston's peach as "broken"?

8. What is the father's role in the story?

9. Why don't the father and the mother try harder?

10. Why does the author have the mother try to persuade the daughter to leave but the father refrain from persuading her to stay?

11. What is Saroyan saying about divorce?

12. At the end of the story does the father feel like Gaston?

13. Is the father using Gaston?

14. Why didn't the father scold his daughter for killing Gaston?

15. What is the significance of the story's title?

CHAPTER

6 Lesson Plan 4

Basic Interpretive Questions

1. Focus: Why do some interpretive questions generate so much more discussion than others? (Brief discussion or journal topic.)

2. Objective: To illustrate and to learn how to write clusters of related interpretive questions (basic questions.)

3. Purpose:
- To increase our mutual understanding (comprehension) and, as a result, our enjoyment of the reading.
- To develop the habit of independent and critical thinking.

4. Input: Review the handout on the four qualities of basic questions and how to develop them. Illustrate the qualities of a basic interpretive question with the basic question on "The Road Not Taken" (According to Frost, has the narrator's choice of the less traveled road been for better or worse?). Emphasize that the question is a real issue because sufficient evidence supports either side. In short, either answer could be correct depending on each individual's interpretations of the poem.

5. Modeling: Have students complete (in pairs) **Exercise 3** on good basic questions. Review questions and individual answers as a class. As needed, discuss disagreements.

6. Closure: Conduct a demonstration discussion of this basic question: Based on this meeting, does Saroyan want us to conclude that the man's daughter has more in common with Gaston than her father? At the end of discussion, students write their individual resolutions to the basic question in a paragraph. Answers must be supported with evidence from the story.

Basic Interpretive Questions

After you have conducted several discussions, you will observe sooner or later that some interpretive questions require you to look at many lines and passages of a reading and give rise to a number of other related questions about the author's meaning. Those interpretive questions that consistently lead to sustained discussion (about thirty minutes per question) are *basic questions.*

Consider the difference between these two questions on William Saroyan's "Gaston." (1) Why does the father refrain from hugging his daughter when she returns to her mother in New York?; and (2) Does Saroyan want us to conclude that the daughter or the father has more in common with Gaston's situation? Both questions are interpretive, but the first is fairly easy to resolve. You could probably find some satisfactory answer just by rereading the conclusion of the story. Since the daughter has made clear she wanted to return to her mother, the father does not want to put a guilt trip on her—that is, make her feel bad about leaving him. Unlike the mother, the father is careful not to manipulate the feelings of his daughter. In contrast, to answer satisfactorily the second question, you would likely have to explore a number of related questions. For example: Why does the father say that Gaston could only *try* to live in their house? Why does the father think it unfair for people to holler when someone comes out of his house? Is the father trying to tell his daughter that she, like Gaston, is "out in the world and on [her] own now"? Why does the girl describe Gaston's house as "broken"? Why does the author imply that the girl is as confused as Gaston? Why does the girl say that her father's house is like Gaston's? Why does the story end with the father feeling only "a little" like the squashed Gaston? And so on. To answer these additional questions, and others you might think of that have something to do with whether the father's or the daughter's situation is more like Gaston's, would obviously take a great deal more time to answer than would the first question about why the father doesn't hug his daughter when she leaves him. In short, the second question is **basic** because it deals with a major issue or problem in the story that requires you to interpret a great deal of the story before you could answer it in a comprehensive and satisfactory way.

Centering discussion on basic questions has two advantages. First, they add a new dimension to thinking about interpretive questions because they require you to organize more facts and ideas to deepen your understanding of the story. Second, basic questions yield a more comprehensive and integrated explanation of the author's meaning than you would have discussing interpretive questions that cover an assortment of unrelated topics or problems about meaning.

But how do you find and write basic questions for discussion? There are two methods:

(1) Begin by choosing any interpretive question that you care about and then try to write a number of questions that are related to it and help explore its implications.
(2) After you have written at least twenty interpretive questions on the reading, look for a pattern or common topic that some of them seem to be related to.

Whether you write a basic question deductively (from the general to the specific (1)) or inductively (from the specific to the general (2)), the goal is to formulate a **cluster** of related questions. Hence, a basic question is defined as *a cluster of at least eight related interpretive questions, each one of which is a distinct problem for discussion.* In short, each sub-question or follow-up question is an aspect or a piece of a comprehensive answer to the basic question. Like all interpretive questions these follow-up questions should have the qualities of any good discussion question.

In short, the basic question is the **problem**, the focus of discussion; the cluster is the co-leaders' **plan** to solve it; and the reading selection is the **source** of information needed to resolve it. The following models—one from the Frost poem, and the other from the Gaston short story—illustrate the characteristics of a good basic question.

"The Road Not Taken"

According to Frost, has the narrator's choice of the less traveled road been for better or worse?

If it has been for the better, then:

1. Why is the title of the poem about the road *not* taken?
2. Why does the narrator wish that he could have taken both roads? (line 2)
3. Why does the narrator say the road less traveled had "perhaps" the better claim? (7)
4. Why is there an exclamation point at the end of line 13?
5. Why does the narrator say that he will be telling us about his choice of the less traveled road with a sigh? (16)
6. Does the last line of the poem refer to a good or bad difference?

If it has been for the worse, then:

7. Does the title of the poem refer to the road less traveled or to the road that most people would have taken?
8. Why does the narrator admit, in retrospect, both roads were really about the same? (10)
9. Why does the narrator say he kept the choice of the first road for another day? (13)
10. Why does the narrator say he will be telling about his choice "ages and ages hence"?
11. Why is there a dash after "I" in line 18?
12. Is the narrator trying to convince himself that he has made the better choice in taking the road less traveled?

"Gaston"

Does Saroyan want us to conclude that the daughter or the father has more in common with Gaston's situation?

If the daughter has more in common with Gaston, then:

1. Why does the father describe Gaston as "the grand *boulevardier*"? (line 34)
2. Does he fail to explain what a grand boulevardier is because he thinks the term applies only to himself? (34, 37)
3. Unlike the girl who wants to squash Gaston because he is ugly, why does the father think he is handsome? (34)
4. Is the father trying to tell his daughter that she, like Gaston, is "out in the world and on [her] own now"? (35)
5. Why does the father say that Gaston could only *try* to live in their house? (35)
6. Why does the father think it unfair for people to holler when someone comes out of his house? (34)
7. Why does the girl describe Gaston's house as "broken"? (37)

If the father has more in common with Gaston, then:

8. Why does the girl ask *who* the bug is rather than *what* it is? (33)
9. Why does the author imply that the girl is as confused as Gaston? (36)
10. Why does the girl begin to adopt her father's view of Gaston? (35–38)
11. Why does the girl cry just before she kills Gaston? (38)

12. Why does the girl say that her father's house is like Gaston's? (38)
13. Near the end of the story, why does Saroyan refer to the father as "the man"? (38)
14. Why does the story end with the father feeling only "a little" like the squashed Gaston? (39)

The following exercise (Exercise 3) will help you and your students test their understanding of the four characteristics of a good basic question: (1) all questions in the cluster are interpretive; (2) all are related to the problem; (3) none are repetitious but each a distinct problem; and (4) the cluster has at least eight questions.

Good Basic Questions

"GASTON" EXERCISE 3

Read these two basic questions:

A *Why does the father let his daughter make up her own mind instead of telling her what to do?*
B *Does the author intend the little girl's situation to be like Gaston's?*

Directions: For each question that follows, put an (A) in front those **related** to the first basic question and a (B) in front of those that are related to the second basic question.

1. Why doesn't the father make plans with his daughter about what they would do?

2. Are we to believe that the girl's home, like Gaston's, can never be in order again because of her parent's divorce?

3. Why does the father answer with questions when his daughter asks if he is going to squash Gaston or holler?

4. Why does the father let his daughter decide whether to go with him to buy a peach or to stay at home?

5. Is the girl "homeless" because her loyalty to her father and mother is divided?

6. Why does everything seem wrong with Gaston just after the mother's phone call?

7. Is the author suggesting that the girl, like Gaston, cannot live happily in her father's house?

8. Why doesn't the father tell the girl what to say if her mother calls except that he has gone to get her a bad peach?

9. Why doesn't the father comment when his daughter says, "I want to be here"?

10. Is the "break" in Gaston's house intended to suggest the break in the girl's life when her parents divorced?

11. Why does the father ask his daughter why she squashed Gaston instead of scolding her?

12. Why does the narrator tell us that Gaston is wandering around confused after the telephone call with the mother?

13. If the little girl's situation is like Gaston's, why does the author have both the girl and her father say that Gaston is like him?

14. Why does the father resist his impulse to hug his daughter as she leaves?

15. Why does the father say only "Oh" when his daughter says she is flying back to New York?

16. What does the girl's crying after she squashed Gaston remind her of when she cried, "long ago"?

Three Levels of Perception: On Writing Questions That Have Real Doubt

To avoid writing and asking questions that lack real doubt in the minds of the co-leaders, they must begin at their deepest level of perception or understanding of the text. To do so, they must sometimes write a question based on an assumption or even a hypothesis (a guess at meaning). In short, not all questions should be neutral or void of any previous understandings or interpretations. The following questions illustrate the three levels of doubt or degrees or perception.

1. **Neutral:** The leaders question the significance of a fact, a detail, an event, the choice of vocabulary, a sentence, or a phrase. (What is the meaning of X?)

   Example:

   Why does the father decide not to hug his daughter as the story ends?

2. **Assumption**: The leaders' question is based on a prior interpretation; the question is not neutral but based on a previous understanding. (Because X seems to be true, how do we explain Y?)

   Example:

   Why does the father respect is daughter's decisions?

3. **Hypothesis:** The leader's question is a guess at meaning or an attempt to explain something in light of something else. The level of doubt here is in the *maybe*—what *may* be true. (Does X explain Y?)

   Example:

   Does the father decline to hug his daughter at the end of the story because he does not want to confuse her feelings?

Note: It is important to distinguish questions based on assumptions or hypotheses from leading questions. Leading questions by definition lack doubt and indicate or hint at the answer expected. Leading questions always have tell-tale words or phrases in them: really, honestly, truly, or a negative. Leading questions, asked so often in courts of law, never have a place in Socratic discussion.

CHAPTER

7 Lesson Plan 5

Spontaneous Follow-up Questions

1. Focus:	What is the difference between a prepared and a spontaneous follow-up question? For example? (Note: a prepared follow-up (cluster questions for a basic question) is always interpretive while spontaneous follow-ups can be factual, interpretive, or even evaluative in special situations (e.g., lack of response).
2. Objective:	To become a good co-leader who listens actively to the answers of participants and asks appropriate follow-up questions.
3. Purpose:	To illustrate the purpose and kinds of good spontaneous follow-up questions and to practice and develop the skills needed to be a good co-leader of discussion.
4. Input:	Explain the purpose and use of different kinds of spontaneous follow-up questions by reviewing the one-page handout in the Guidelines.
5. Modeling, checking, and guided practice:	Have students complete (in pairs or individually) **Exercise 4** on follow-up questions. Review individual answers as a class. Emphasize that there is no such thing as a perfect follow-up to a response; *any follow-up is satisfactory as long as* it gets a participant (or another participant) to reflect on and develop the answer. An unsatisfactory follow-up ignores the answer and goes on to another idea.
6. Closure:	Review the summary sheet on how to handle common problems in discussion: Scenarios of Discussion Review.

Spontaneous Follow-up Questions

> "The role of the teacher is to uncover the question that the answer hides."
>
> J. Baldwin

Why do some discussions fail even when you know the group has read carefully and that you began with a good interpretive question? Without doubt, such discussions so often fall flat, go nowhere, become chaotic, or degenerate into bull sessions because the leader(s) do not listen to what they hear. As a result, they miss opportunity after opportunity to follow-up on the ideas of the participants. A further consequence is that because answers are not developed, no one has any sense of satisfaction or gain in understanding.

The chief role of the co-leaders in discussion is to direct traffic, that is, to direct and control the flow of ideas among the participants. Co-leaders fulfill this role by introducing **prepared** questions to initiate discussion, basic or otherwise, **and** by asking **spontaneous** follow-up questions **to develop** and **to connect** ideas that help solve the problem(s) under discussion. By following these guidelines, you will lead an effective discussion that increases your own and the group's understanding of the reading. As a result, you will also increase your mutual enjoyment of the reading, the ultimate goal of the Socratic Seminar.

1. If you remember that there is no such thing as a perfect or ideal follow-up question, you will not make your role more difficult by trying to second-guess yourself. In other words, there are several distinct kinds of follow-up questions that could be asked at any given moment of discussion. *The kind of follow-up question asked in a specific situation depends on the leader's purpose.*

   Is it (a) **to clarify**? Example: "What did you mean when you said ____?" or "Could you explain more of what you mean by ____?"

   Is it (b) **to substantiate**? Example: "Upon what in the reading are you basing your answer?" or "How do you know? What in the reading gave you that impression?"

   Is it (c) **to get more opinion**? Example: "Maria, do you agree with John's idea that ____? If so, could you explain? If not, why do you disagree?

   Is it (d) **to test for consistency**? Example: "Sarah, if what you say is correct, then how do you explain ____?"

   Is it (e) **to relate** a response to the prepared question? Example: "Brian, how does what you have said help answer our question about ____?"

Is it (f) **to draw out the implications** of a response? Example: "Ryan, are you saying ____?" "By X do you mean Y?"

Or finally, is it (g) **to resolve** the prepared question? Example: "John, at this time what is your best answer to our question about ____? Or, "Laura, what different answers have you heard so far to our basic question?"

2. Many more ideas are heard in discussion than can ever be pursued or developed. It is unrealistic, pointless, and even impossible to try to keep track of everything that is said in discussion. (It simply cannot be done unless you record your discussions. I can recommend no better way to improve your leadership skills and those of your students than to record a discussion and then to critique it later.)
3. As a result, co-leaders must make conscious **choices** about what they want to: (a) pursue, (b) table, or (c) ignore in any given response or series of responses. In short, the leaders' responsibility is to make choices which guide or direct the discussion—that is, that keep the responses of the participants relevant to the prepared question(s) presently on the floor.
4. How often must a leader make a choice about what to pursue, to table, or to ignore? Experience shows that the co-leaders must ask an **average** of one follow-up question **for every two or three responses**. Unless the leaders maintain this average by asking enough follow-up questions, discussion soon reverts to a series of random, unrelated, off-the-cuff comments characteristic of mundane conversation.
5. Following these guidelines leads to two important conclusions. First, good discussion **does not** consist in asking the "right" or perfect follow-up question at the "right" time since there is no such thing **but rather** in the effectiveness of the overall **pattern** of the follow-up questions asked. Second, the co-leaders' role in discussion is **to develop** and **to connect** the ideas of the participants to the prepared questions under consideration. In this way, resolution is achieved, new insights discovered, and enjoyment increased.

Guidelines: Spontaneous Follow-up Questions

The chief role of the co-leaders in discussion is to direct traffic—that is, to direct and control the flow of ideas among the participants. Co-leaders fulfill this role by introducing **prepared** questions to initiate discussion, basic or otherwise, **and** by asking **spontaneous** follow-up questions **to develop** and **to connect** ideas that help solve the problems under discussion. By following these guidelines, you will lead an effective discussion that increases your own and the group's understanding of the reading. As a result, you will also increase your mutual enjoyment of the reading, the ultimate goal of shared inquiry.

1. If you remember that there is no such thing as a perfect or ideal follow-up question, you will not make your role more difficult by trying to second-guess yourself. In other words, there are several distinct kinds of follow-up questions that could be asked at any given moment of discussion. The kind of follow-up question asked in a specific situation depends on the leader's **purpose**.

   Is it (a) *to clarify?* (for example: "What did you mean when you said _____?" or "Could you explain more of what you meant by _____?")
   Is it (b) *to substantiate*? (for example: "Upon what in the text are you basing your answer?" or "How do you know? What in the text gave your that impression?")
   Is it (c) to *get more opinion*? (for example: "Maria, do you agree with John's view that _____? If so, could you explain? If not, why do you disagree?")
   Is it (d) to *test for consistency*? (for example: "Maria, if what you say is correct, how do you explain _____?")
   Is it (e) *to relate* a response to the prepared question? (for example: "Maria, how does what you have just said help answer our question about _____?")
   Or, finally, is it (f) *to resolve* the question under discussion? (for example: "Brian, what now is your best answer to our question about _____?" or "Lisa, how many answers have you heard to our question?")

2. Many more ideas are heard in discussion than can ever be pursued or developed. It is unrealistic, pointless, and even impossible to try to keep track of *everything* that is said in discussion. It simply cannot be done unless you record your discussion with a view to improving your leadership.
3. Hence, the co-leaders must make conscious **choices** about what: (a) to pursue, (b) to table, or (c) to ignore in any given response or series of responses. In short, the leaders' responsibility is to make choices that guide or direct

the discussion—that is, that keep the responses of the participants relevant to the prepared question(s) presently on the floor.

4. How often must a leader make a choice about what to pursue, to table, or to ignore? Experience shows that the co-leaders must ask an **average** of one follow-up question *for every two or three responses.* Unless the leaders maintain this average, discussion soon reverts to a series of random, unrelated, off-the-cuff comments characteristic of mundane conversation.
5. These guidelines lead to two important conclusions. First, good discussion does **not** consist in asking the "right" or perfect follow-up question at the "right" time since there is no such thing **but rather** in the effectiveness of the overall **pattern** of the follow-up questions asked. Second, the co-leaders' role in discussion is **to develop** and **to connect** the ideas of the participants to the prepared questions under consideration.

The following practice exercise on follow-up questions (on the next page for easy copying and handout) on "Gaston" will help you to understand and illustrate for your students the kinds and purposes of good follow-up questions. The purpose of this exercise is to help you and your students to think about how they (as co-leaders) would deal with common situations that often come up in discussion. For example, what follow-up question could a leader ask when: (1) there is no response at all; (2) the response ignores the question; (3) the response has multiple ideas; (4) the response is wrong; (5) the participant does not understand the question; (6) the response is incoherent (not clear); or (7) the participant tries to dismiss the question because he/she doesn't want to think about it?

Spontaneous Follow-up Questions

"GASTON" EXERCISE 4

Directions: Each group below consists of a question and a response during discussion. After each response, write in what you consider to be a good follow-up question. Remember the purpose of any follow-up question (which can be factual, interpretive, or even evaluative) is to get the participant **to reflect** on his or her answer so that the co-leaders help him or her **to develop it**.

1.

Leader: Why does the mother try to persuade her daughter to leave but the father tells her only that the important thing is what she wants?

Sarah: Because the mother is selfish and more involved with her own feelings. She doesn't even realize that it might be better for her daughter to live with her father. But I wonder why the girl wanted a rotten peach.

Follow-up question:

2.

Leader: Is the author implying that the girl's house, like Gaston's, can never be put in order again because of her parents' divorce?

Brian: For sure. Divorce can be tough on some people.

Follow-up question:

3.

Leader: Why does the father answer with a question when the girl asks if he is going to squash Gaston?

Rachael: What questions?

Follow-up question:

4.

Leader: Near the end of the story, why does Saroyan refer to the father as "the man"?

John: I don't have a clue. Call on somebody else. Anyway, who cares?

Follow-up question:

5.

Leader: Why does the father resist the impulse to hug his daughter when she leaves to return to her mother?

Laura: He really doesn't love her at all. She was just something he got rid of.

Follow-up question:

6.

Leader: Why does the mother ridicule the girl's father but he says nothing bad about the mother?

Chris: Because that's what the story is all about.

Follow-up question:

7.

Leader: Why does no one in the story have a name except for Gaston?

Shanice: Her father wants to be entertaining. He's a fun kinda guy.

Follow-up question:

8.

Leader: Why does the girl ask her father why it is important for her to be where she wants to be?

Linda: I'll bet that question never occurred to her as being important before that moment.

Marc: She's probably so confused by this time that she really doesn't understand her situation.

Dave: Maybe she wants to see if her father would react like her mother. She did ask him what she should say if her mother called when he was gone.

Follow-up question:

Scenarios of Discussion Review: How to Handle Common Problems

1. **No response at all** (which is not uncommon in early discussions). **Six solutions**: (a) *repeat* the question to give the participant time to think; (b) *rephrase* the question to give the student time to think; (c) ask a related *factual* question; (d) ask a related *interpretive* question; (e) ask a related question of *evaluation*; or (f) as a last resort, call on another student.
2. **Answer is unsupported** (an opinion) **or an evaluation based on experience or personal values. Three solutions**: (a) ask for textual evidence; (b) ask a follow-up question on that evidence; or (c) ask another student to agree or disagree.
3. **When a student does not understand the question:** rephrase it or ask another student to explain it.
4. **When the response ignores the question** (not uncommon in early discussions when students may have trouble focusing): repeat the question.
5. **When the answer is not clear** (not uncommon in early discussions for students who are not accustomed to explaining their ideas in a group). Without intimidation, the *leader must get clarification.* For example, "Maria, could you explain more of what you meant by _____?"
6. **A wrong answer**—that is, an interpretation that cannot be supported by evidence or that is contradicted by other evidence. **Three solutions**: (a) ask for supporting textual evidence that _____; (b) ask someone else if they agree (if they agree, ask for evidence); (c) ask a follow-up question for consistency—for example: "If that is so, how do you explain _____?" (Note: The leader must not try "to help" the students by telling them that they are wrong. To do so, makes them wonder when they will be corrected next and, as a result, dampens future responses, or, just as bad, the leader becomes the authority *when the only authority in discussion is the text.* In short, participants must learn to judge for themselves, as in life, which answers are right or wrong, satisfactory, good, better, or best.)
7. **Multiple responses: Three solutions**: (a) follow-up on one of them but do not ignore them all by merely calling on another student; pursue whatever seems the most interesting or relevant to you; (b) table, on your seating chart, one or two ideas that you do not immediately pursue, but come back to them later; (c) ask another student if they agree with _____. The leader's role is to develop and connect answers to the basic question, not merely to invite students to speak by calling on them by name.

8. **Assumption in the prepared question is challenged** (more common when students become more independent thinkers). **Three solutions:** (a) ask for supporting evidence from the text; (b) get another opinion; or (c) ask a follow-up question about the evidence from the text for your assumption.

CHAPTER

8 Lesson Plan 6

Preparing Students For Discussion

1. **Focus:**	What questions do you have at this moment about co-leading a discussion? Brief discussion.
2. **Objective:**	To answer your questions about co-leading. To dispel student doubts about being good co-leaders. To develop their confidence as co-leaders.
3. **Purpose:**	To prepare you to be effective co-leaders so that everyone will increase their understanding and enjoyment of the readings.
4. **Input:**	o Review the Four Rules of Socratic Discussion. o Review Guidelines for co-leading. o Review Use and Importance of Seating Chart. o Review Guidelines for Preparing Questions. o Review Guidelines for Spontaneous Questions. o Review Criteria for Critique of Discussion.
5. **Modeling:**	With a teacher or student co-leader, conduct a twenty-minute demonstration discussion of a poem. Suggestion: W. H. Auden, "The Unknown Citizen."
6. **Checking:**	Review the demonstration discussion by having students raise questions about how the ten criteria from the critique sheet were or were not applied.
7. **Guided practice:**	Review the demonstration discussion by having students suggest ways that the discussion could have been improved.
8. **Closure:**	Do you still have any questions about co-leading that were not answered satisfactorily?

What is a Socratic Seminar?

"The role of the teacher is to uncover the question that the answer hides."
James Baldwin

The Seminar is a series of extended discussions focused on a single topic, theme(s), or series of readings that may or may not be related. The Seminar is conducted by a teacher, a teacher-team, or co-led by students who have been trained in the Socratic method of learning (Lessons 1–6). Its usual length is a full class period of sixty or ninety minutes, three to five days a week.

Before students begin to co-lead discussions, an entire period should be given to review an explanation of these fundamentals: The Criteria for Choosing Texts for Socratic Discussion (pages 74–76) to be sure that co-leaders understand the purpose of each rule—particularly the rule about asking only questions.

The Guidelines for Co-leading Socratic Discussion (page 60) must also be reviewed to ensure that students clearly understand their role and the purpose of discussion. Before discussion, student co-leaders must meet to refine and agree upon the questions that they plan to use in their discussion of the day's assigned reading. See Guidelines for Pre-discussion (page 63).

An important part of the Guidelines for Discussion that must also be reviewed in preparation for Lesson 6 is the Use and Importance of the Seating Chart.

Finally, students must understand that discussion will be evaluated in three ways: (1) the teacher's completion of the Criteria for Critique of Discussion (page 62) during the meeting; (2) an oral and/or written resolution of the basic question(s) at the end of the discussion; and/or (3) a formal follow-up essay (due a few days later) on one of the basic questions or commentaries on four of ten key quotations from the text, that explains its context (who and when) and theme (overall meaning.)

Since the Seminars often make use of one or more available film versions, this sequence is recommended:

1. On day one, begin with a review of the cast of characters of the poem, short story, novel, or play and then follow up with a few opening scenes of the film to associate the main characters with a face in the minds of the student audience.
2. Before viewing each of the following scenes of the story, begin with a plot-check quiz of the *first reading*. After viewing the video of each act, students do a *second reading* and then write interpretive questions in pairs, as co-leaders. See Guidelines for Writing About Film (page 58).

3. The Seminar itself is always a full-period discussion of two to four basic interpretive questions, which may take more than one day depending on the time allowed (60, 90, or 120 minutes). In the beginning, the teacher(s) conduct(s) *demonstration discussions* to model what will be expected of the students when they co-lead. In the following Seminar discussions, to ensure that time is not wasted on questions that are not basic, clear, and specific, the teacher assigns each pair of co-leaders one of the approved basic questions from the lesson plan and then has them write eight to ten prepared follow-up questions directly related to the problem of interpretation. Each prepared follow-up question must be documented with a specific reference (act, scene, and line in a play, page reference in short stories or novels, and line in a poem) to allow the group, during discussion, to get into textual analysis. At the end of discussion, students hand in their prepared follow-up questions (one paper with two names) for a teacher grade or revision.

Resolution and Evaluation

4. The Seminar concludes in two ways:
   (a) With an **oral resolution** after about twenty to thirty minutes of discussion on each of four basic questions (about one to two hours). The co-leaders:
   - repeat the basic interpretive question
   - call on members to repeat the answers they remember hearing
   - check if anyone in the group has an answer* that has not yet been repeated, or discussed in the first place
   - have each member of the group compose their final answer (orally or in writing)
   - ask members to identify memorable ideas heard during discussion that led them to develop their thinking, change their mind, and revise their initial answer to form their final conclusion.

   (b) With **written resolution**—an essay exam that is either half-page commentaries on four of ten key quotations of the novel, short story, poem, or play **or** a resolution in class to one of the basic questions previously discussed.

*Note: At the beginning of discussion the co-leaders state the basic question and gives the group at least five minutes to write down an initial answer *to give them time to think.* As elementary as this practice should be to any teacher, without giving the group time to gather their thoughts, discussion too often begins with: "I don't know"; "Because that's the way the author wrote it"; "To make money" and other flippant nonsense that sets the wrong tone. The second reason for having the group write down an initial answer is that it enables them to recall it and bring it up during the resolution activity.

Guidelines for Discussion and Writing about Film

Exercise 1: Make notations on what is important, what you do not understand, what you particularly liked (emotionally) and/or disliked, and on what is related (one part of the original story to another), making connections.

Exercise 2: Make notations on what has been *added*, *omitted*, and *retained* from the original story.

Exercise 3: List ten *important differences* between the movie and the short story, play, or the novel.

Exercise 4: List ten *important similarities* between the movie and the short story, play, or the novel.

Guidelines for Exercises 3 and 4

1. Each difference or similarity between the movie and the text (short story, play, or novel) must be written <u>*as a complete sentence*</u>.
2. In each sentence, refer to *both* the movie and the story.
3. *No two sentences may begin the same way*; the sentence openings must be varied.
4. Number each difference or similarity and skip a line between each sentence.
5. Circle the numbers of what you regard as the three most important differences or similarities. *Rank in order of importance.*
6. Use ink (no pencil, ever), write on standard paper (no spiral, ever), and put the proper heading on the upper right-hand corner.
7. Avoid wordiness; try to be as concise as possible. Use active voice.

Glue Words for "differences"

but, however, unlike, in contrast, although, as if, on the other hand, still, nevertheless, yet, rather than, despite, in spite of, instead of, contrary to

Glue Words for "similarities"

similarly, in like manner, just as, in the same way, like, as, equally, similar to

Glue Words for "ranking"

first, second, finally, more importantly, most importantly, another, furthermore, moreover, in addition, again, of primary importance, the least, the greatest

Models

1. Unlike the emphatic conclusion of Faulkner's "Barn Burning" ("He did not look back)," in the film version, Sarty looks back as he sees his family moving on to another farm.
2. Like the novel, the film version of *The Great Gatsby* portrays Nick Carraway as attracted to and yet repelled by Gatsby's character and values.

Seminar

GUIDELINES FOR CO-LEADING

When you co-lead a fifteen minute discussion of an assigned reading, please follow these **guidelines** to insure that discussion is truly shared inquiry.

1. Sit next to your co-leader and make out a **seating chart** from your position in the group.
2. Have the group **write down** your prepared question, basic or otherwise, on a piece of paper and give them two or three minutes to jot down a brief, initial response. Participants need time to think and to note ideas that they may wish to bring up later in discussion.
3. Observe the **four rules of Socratic discussion**. *Remember it is vital that you and your co-leader limit yourselves to asking only questions.* You must avoid statements of any kind. Unless you do so, the group will begin looking to you for approval or even disapproval and drift away from thinking for themselves. Indeed, whenever a leader begins making statements, however well intentioned, the discussion soon becomes a disguised lecture or it may even revert to an argument.
4. Begin the discussion by calling on someone **by name** to give his or her answer. You must address all questions by name to control the flow of discussion. Although participants may speak up freely without being called upon, you must recognize them by name to direct the group's attention.
5. Make every effort to **call on everyone** in your group at least once or twice. Put a mark next to the name on your seating chart every time that you call on someone to respond. Try to avoid the extremes of calling on the same few participants too often or of not calling on someone at all.
6. **For every two or three responses**, you and your co-leader should be asking a spontaneous follow-up question to develop the ideas given and to keep the group's thinking focused on your prepared question.
7. At the end of fifteen minutes (minimum) or thirty minutes (maximum), ask your group to recall briefly the different answers that have been given to your prepared question. Note these answers briefly on your seating chart and hand in at the end of class.
8. The answers to your prepared question noted on your seating chart are the degree to which you have increased your own and the group's understanding of the reading. This is **resolution**, which is an individual matter (not group consensus or truth by vote).

Importance and Use of the Seating Chart

At the beginning of each discussion, it is important that co-leaders make a seating chart from their position in the group, which is seated in a circle. The seating chart has three important functions:

1. **It locates each participant and enables the co-leaders to call on each one by name. Preface all questions by name.**
   - This helps you to control the discussion.
   - If all have responsibility for a question, usually, none do.
   - It gives the person called on a few seconds to think of an answer. In theory, everyone should be prepared to speak all the time, but in practice, it seldom happens.
   - It enables you to call on those less likely to speak up on their own. Throwing a question out to everyone usually results in the verbally aggressive taking over the discussion.
2. **It enables the co-leaders to involve all participants more or less equally.**
   - During a twenty to thirty minute segment of discussion, the co-leaders should try to call on everyone at least once, ideally twice.
   - The co-leaders should ask an average of one follow-up question for every two or three responses.
3. **It enables the co-leaders to exercise their three options: to ignore, to table, or to pursue responses.**
   - Next to the names of the participants, the co-leaders can jot down those ideas they pursue immediately and table those for later discussion.
   - Because it is impossible to follow-up on every idea in discussion, co-leaders must make a conscious choice about what they pursue immediately, table for later, or ignore. Unless they do so, they will begin to tag end—to pick up on the last remark of the last participant. When this happens, discussion becomes mundane conversation.

Seminar

CRITERIA FOR CRITIQUE OF A DISCUSSION

Co-leaders: ____________________ and ____________________

English ____

Reading ______________________________ Date __________

Question: ______________________________________

____

____

Code: Good (10) Pretty good (5) Needs improvement (0)

1. Did the leaders initiate discussion by beginning with a **good interpretive question?**	10	5	0
2. Did the leaders call on **all** participants at least once?	10	5	0
3. Did the leaders **average** one follow-up question for every two or three responses?	10	5	0
4. Did the leaders **avoid making statements** or asking leading questions?	10	5	0
5. Did the leaders seek **clarification** as well as **substantiation** when necessary?	10	5	0
6. Did the leaders **co-lead**? Did they share equally the task of asking follow-up questions?	10	5	0
7. Did the leaders get answers to **questions on the floor** before moving on to new ideas?	10	5	0
8. Did the leaders **stick to** their prepared question?	10	5	0
9. Did the leaders **pick up ideas** from the participants for follow-up questions or did they rely too much on their list of prepared follow-up questions?	10	5	0
10. Did the leaders **resolve** their prepared question?	10	5	0

Guidelines for Pre-discussion

PREPARING DISCUSSION QUESTIONS WITH YOUR CO-LEADER

1. Before meeting with your co-leader, each of you should have written fifteen to twenty interpretive questions with a page reference for each. Page references make it easy for both of you to turn to that part of the text that gave you the idea for the question. Page references also assure you that your question is specific.
2. Begin pre-discussion by checking the wording of your questions. Do this by applying the Checklist for Qualities of Good Discussion Questions. If you cannot revise a question to fit these six characteristics, drop it. If you have trouble getting to your deepest level of understanding (writing questions that have real doubt for you), review "Three Levels of Perception: On Writing Questions That Have Real Doubt" (Chapter 6, page 44).
3. At this point you should decide if you want to go with a list of at least ten good interpretive questions (arranged in any order that seems logical to you) or decide on writing a basic question similar to those that you have found in the following lesson plans at the end of this lesson. Indeed, you may want to try out one of the suggested basic questions that lack prepared follow-up questions to see if together you can come up with a cluster of at least eight questions of your own.
4. Agree upon the question that you want to use to open your discussion. Do not be overly concerned with your choice of an opening question. Any question that you both genuinely care about will be suitable.

PART

II

Socratic Seminars

CHAPTER

9 Socratic Seminars and Film

An Overview: Great Books Common Core Curriculum

This course applies the Socratic method of teaching and learning to a series of Seminar discussions that focus not only on select readings but also on comparison–contrast discussions of film versions of those readings. We do so because a movie version of a story is itself an interpretation with which its author may or may not agree. As a result, new interpretations often arise that would not otherwise have been considered and our understanding and enjoyment of a story is increased.

This course is also a balance of contemporary authors: Carson McCullers, William Saroyan, Ray Bradbury, Neil Postman, Kate DiCamillo, Judy Blume, Hans Kung, Gina Berriault, President Obama, and Gene Siskel, and members of the greatest faculty in the world—authors of the Great Books of the Western World: Abraham Lincoln, Khalil Gibran, William Saroyan, William Faulkner, Kurt Vonnegut, Ralph Waldo Emerson, and William Shakespeare.

Why Great Books and these established contemporary authors? Why these Great Books? Great Books, according to Matthew Arnold, are "the best that is known and thought in the world." G. K. Chesterton maintains that Great Books are always relevant because they are timeless—they can be read and reinterpreted by each succeeding generation in light of its own experience. Great Books are those common core books that generation after generation read and reread because of their universal themes and issues, boundless interpretations, inspired and memorable language, and timeless wisdom. In short, some books become great because they endure. And they endure because the human race endures.

Chapter 10: Lesson Plans 7 and 8: How Important is a Girlfriend, a Brother, or a Parent in Your Life?

Carson McCullers "Sucker" illustrates the futility of a high school romance that leads to the estrangement of two brothers, Pete and Sucker. "Sucker" became the title character because he became Pete's twelve-year-old stepbrother as a baby when his parents were killed in an auto accident. Because he was so young, Sucker soon became part of the family of Pete and his kid sisters. Sucker got his nickname because he always remembered and believed whatever Pete said. However, Pete and Sucker's close relationship changed when Pete, a sixteen-year-old high school sophomore, became obsessed with winning the attention of an eighteen-year-old senior, Maybelle Watts. Strangely, there seemed to be a direct connection between these two relationships: when Pete and Maybelle got along so did Peter and Sucker but when problems arose, both relationships soured. And that's what bothers Pete. As he tells his story in retrospect, he is still trying to figure out why he lost Maybelle and, more importantly, his brother Sucker. Hence, the story raises this basic question of interpretation: Does Pete look back on his relationship with Maybelle to find a solution to their breakup or to excuse his cruel behavior towards Sucker?

During World War II, when **William Faulkner** was at the apex of his career as a national author, he wrote **"Two Soldiers"** and its sequel, **"Shall Not Perish."** Both stories are told from the viewpoint of a nine-year-old narrator—Pete's brother. In "Two Soldiers," much to the dismay of his anxious parents, nineteen-year-old Pete is determined to join the US Army. And his little brother is just as determined to join him—regardless of his age. Indeed, Willie (in the movie) runs away from home and begins walking the thirty miles to the Army recruiting station in Memphis. When these two brothers find each other, only then do they realize the depth of their brotherhood. Basic question: Why does Faulkner regard Willie as much a soldier as his brother Pete?

The sequel to "Two Soldiers," "Shall Not Perish," is a title that anyone who has memorized the most renowned speech of our 16th President, would recognize immediately as an allusion to Abraham Lincoln's Address at Gettysburg. According to Pulitzer Prize winner, Gary Wills, The Gettysburg Address was "the words that changed America." When Lincoln proclaimed that our nation was "dedicated to the proposition that all men are created equal," he so shocked some biased Chicago journalists, one of them expressed his self-righteous disgust in the next edition of the *Chicago Tribune*, November 20, 1863.

"Are You a Bumper-Sticker Patriot?" echoes Thomas Paine's bitter ridicule of the "sunshine patriot" of our Revolutionary War. Like Faulkner in his "Shall Not Perish," **President Obama** gave our nation a profound reminder on the meaning of authentic patriotism today in his speech at Independence, Missouri, June 30, 2008.

Chapter 11: Lesson Plan 9: Is Technology as Much a Curse as a Blessing?

While **Isaac Asimov** is nearly always optimistic and a firm believer in the inevitable progress of technology (as in ***Robbie*** in the high school book), Ray Bradbury's vision of the future of technology is always skeptical, cautionary and even alarming. In "**The Veldt**," George Hadley, the father of Peter and Wendy, marvels at the mechanical genius who had conceived their Happy Life Home. However, he does begin to worry somewhat that his children have become obsessed with one room, the nursery. Lydia, his wife, is far more concerned than he about their children's mental health. Indeed, she believes that the nursery has become a surrogate parent. Their ten-year-old son tells his father that he hates him when he realizes that he plans to shut down the nursery and take the family on vacation. Wendy, Peter's twin sister, is just as dependent and obsessed with the nursery. In an attempt to solve their concern that family life is becoming dysfunctional, George turns to David McClean, a psychologist, for analysis of the nursery and advice about how he can help his children who are as out of control as the nursery seems to be. The story raises a genuine basic question: Even after the Hadleys realize that the nursery is a real danger, why are they unable to do anything to improve their family life?

Nonfiction readings: When asked why teachers use his stories and books, Ray Bradbury replied:

> Because I speak in tongues. I write metaphors. Every one of my stories is a metaphor you can remember. The great religions are all metaphors too. We appreciate things like Daniel, the lion's den, you know. People remember those metaphors because they are so vivid; you can't get free of them, and that's what kids like in school. . . . All my life I've been running through the fields picking up bright objects. I turn them over and say, 'Hey, there's a story.'

In a CNN interview when Ray Bradbury spoke spontaneously about **On God, Monsters, and Angels**, he spoke for the first time about the role of religion in his life: "I sit there and cry because I haven't done any of this," he told Sam Weller, his biographer and friend. "It's a God-given thing, and I'm so grateful, so, so grateful. The best description of my career as a writer is, 'At play in the fields of the Lord.'"

"**What Will Our Homes Look Like in 2114**" by Nikki Sheehan is piece of nonfiction that Bradbury himself would have extrapolated from his story of the "Happy Life Home" in "The Veldt" had he lived longer.

Chapter 12: Lesson Plan 10: Is the Desire to Excel as Strong as the Tendency to be Mediocre?

"The Year was 2081, and everybody was finally equal. They weren't only equal before God and the law. They were equal every which way. Nobody was smarter than anybody else. Nobody was better looking than anybody else. Nobody was stronger or quicker than anybody else. All this equality was due to the 211th, 212th, and 213th Amendments to the Constitution, and to the unceasing vigilance of agents of the United States Handicapper General."

So begins the first paragraph of Kurt Vonnegut's renowned "**Harrison Bergeron**," which sets up the context of the entire story. Fourteen-year-old Harrison Bergeron who is seven feet tall, a genius, extraordinarily handsome, athletic, strong, and fearless, wants to live as an unimpeded human being free of government laws that have been designed to create equality for the whole of American society. The story raises two basic questions of interpretation: Is the desire to excel as strong as the tendency to be mediocre? and, Why does Vonnegut regard a movement toward total equality as a threat to our society? Of the four movie versions of his story, Vonnegut approves only the 2006 version: "I am glad to see the appropriate measures have been taken with my story." Nevertheless, some critics prefer the 2009 version. Although the movie ***2081*** follows closely Vonnegut's original story, it makes several radical plot changes that Vonnegut would not likely approve. These differences will be one of our comparison-contrast discussion topics.

For the nonfiction reading, following the guidelines and model in Lesson Plan 10, students write a commentary on the **Shakespeare quotation** from *Twelfth Night* (2.3.146): "Some are born great, some achieve greatness, and some have greatness thrust upon them."

"An Age of Distraction: Digital Deficit Disorder" asks students to find parallels in our age of DDD that are prefigured in the handicaps of Vonnegut's 2081 world of total equality. In a writing assignment students write a report on their 24-hour electronic media fast outlined in the article.

Chapter 13: Lesson Plan 11: Who Are Your Real Friends?

Kate DiCamillo's title ***Because of Winn-Dixie*** suggests that because of Opal's adoption of a stray dog, all of the motley characters in the story are unwittingly led into most unlikely bonds of friendship. In her novel and the movie version of ***Because of Winn-Dixie***, **Kate DiCamillo's** ten-year-old narrator, Opal, early on talks to God about how lonely she is in Naomi, Florida because even the kids she knows—the Dunlap brothers, Amanda Wilkinson, and Sweetie Pie

Thomas—don't want to be her friend. However, because of Winn-Dixie, Opal soon makes several unusual friends. Her quest for friendship raises a basic question about who our real friends are and how it could be that people as unique as Miss Fanny Block, the librarian, Gloria Dump, the neighborhood "witch," Otis, an ex-con, pinched-nose Amanda Wilkinson, and five-year-old Sweetie Pie Thomas, all became genuine friends of Opal. But why? In spite of their many differences, what do they have in common? Although the movie is ninety-five percent faithful to DiCamillo's story, so much so that there can be no question she would approve it, there are four notable differences that raise these questions: (1) Why does the movie open with Opal pretending to play baseball with herself?; (2) Why is the role of Mr. Alfred, manager of Friendly Corners Trailer Park, developed into a major character?; (3) Why is a police officer added to harass Otis as well as the children?; and (4) Why is the preacher's prayer over the food at Gloria and Opal's party moved to the concluding scene?

"**Bad Characters**" by **Jean Stafford** focuses on a bizarre and humorous temporary friendship between an articulate, sharp-witted rich girl and a bold, self-confident poor girl who has made shoplifting a game as well as a way of life. Emily Vanderpool and Lottie Jump are the "bad characters" in Jean Stafford's spellbinding story. (We provide a link to this story so you can access it online.) Of herself Emily says: "I had a bad character, I know that, but my badness never gave me half the enjoyment Jack and Stella [her older brother and sister] thought it did." In contrast, Lottie Jump, Emily's new-found friend got plenty of enjoyment from her "badness." Their most unlikely relationship raises four basic questions: (1) Why is Emily fascinated with as well as revolted by Lottie Jump?; (2) What is the difference between Emily's "badness" and Lottie's?; (3) Does Stafford intend her story to be *entirely* comical and satirical?; and (4) Does Stafford give Emily such a sophisticated (grown-up) vocabulary because she is telling the story in retrospect as an adult?

Does Lottie Jump shoplift only because she is poor? While that may be one reason for some, a study by the Sacramento County Sheriff's department, **"Why Do People Shoplift?"** concludes that motivations vary as much as individuals and circumstances. For those who would like to follow up DiCamillo's story about unlikely friendships with a nonfiction reading, **"Who Are Your Real Friends?"** can apply the characteristics of genuine friendship to those in the novel.

Chapter 14: Lesson Plan 12: How Important is God in Your life?

When I asked my neighbor this question, his prompt reply was, the "Great Spirit" of Chief Joseph. When I asked another neighbor he replied: "Which God? God is a generic word, isn't it? And since it means the supreme being, there can be only one supreme being. God. Right?" Yes of course, I replied.

Let me rephrase the question. Which one and only God do you believe in? Again, he replied promptly. "Jesus is Lord! Son of God the Father and His Holy Spirit." When I asked another neighbor the same question, he recited the Shama: "Hear, O Israel: the Lord our God, the Lord is [the only] One." And, as expected, a Muslim at school told me, "There is no God but Allah and Mohammed his prophet."

Are these but different names for the same God? In short, are the various world religions but different paths to the same God who wears different masks? There are as many who want to believe that as there are those who vehemently affirm that their god is the only god (Martin Buber) and that all others are false. And rightly so. How can there be more than only one true God? A related question inevitably arises: Why is it that some people are so passionate, indeed consumed, about seeking God, while others are indifferent, apathetic, uninterested, and in a word, unaware of any need for God? In his recently published *Do You Believe?*, New York filmmaker Antonio Monda conducts a series of candid interviews with eighteen cultural icons that range from Jane Fonda and Spike Lee to Martin Scorsese and Elie Wiesel. He asks each to reply to five basic questions: Do you believe in God? If so, what is your image of God? What happens to you after death? Do you pray? and Do you think religious believers are deluded? Responses range from Yes and No to Well . . .?

In ***Are You There God? It's Me, Margaret***, **Judy Blume** focuses on the personal dilemma forced upon Margaret to choose between her grandparents' traditional Jewish religion and her parents' Christian faith. Although Margaret has a healthy personal relationship with God whom she confides in during the events of her daily life, her grandparents and parents anger her in that they expect her to choose their religion. In the end, she refuses to do either and returns to God asking forgiveness for having stopped praying to Him—"It wasn't Your fault."

Nonfiction: Hans Kung, in a precis of his "**Why I am Still a Christian**," explains that his Christian faith is not blind and irrational but based on reasonable facts. Equally personal, Debbie Friedman poignantly witnesses her faith in **"Why I am a Jew."**

Chapter 15: Lesson Plan 14: How Does a Someone Cope with a Death in the Family?

The title of this chapter alludes to the title of **James Agee**'s Pulitzer Prize winning autobiographical novel of 1957, ***A Death in the Family***. In Part III (Chapters 14–20) seven-year-old Rufus poignantly recounts the sudden, accidental death of his loving father. The story raises several basic interpretive questions for Socratic discussion: How do Rufus and Catherine cope with the sudden death of their father? Why does Rufus reject the explanation that his father died because God put him to sleep and took him home? Why does Rufus feel so guilty about telling his classmates "My Daddy's dead"? How does Uncle Andrew help Rufus cope with the sudden death of his father? Why does Uncle Andrew tell Rufus that the miraculous butterfly has "more of God in him than that priggish, mealy-mouthed son of a bitch [Father Jackson]"? And why does Agee reveal that Rufus understands more about his father's death than what he is told?

The 1963 DVD, ***All the Way Home*** (title taken from the last sentence of the novel) runs 107 min and is in black and white. In 2002, PBS Masterpiece Theatre televised its own version of ***A Death in the Family***.

Gina Berriault's "The Stone Boy" recounts the poignant story of a ten-year-old boy who accidentally kills his older brother, Eugene, on their way back to pick peas on their farm. Because Arnold delays for some time and does not return promptly home for help, he becomes a "stone boy" apparently devoid of grief. Even his parents and close relatives do not know how to reach out to the traumatized boy. When Arnold does finally turn to his mother at night, she sharply turns him away, evidently unable to cope with her own pain. When she realizes her mistake, and "humbly" asks her son why he knocked at her door at night, he replies flatly, "I didn't want nothing." Berriault then concludes her grim story with this line: "Then he went out the door and down the back steps, his legs trembling from the fright his answer gave him." When asked in an interview if she was pleased with the screenplay, Berriault replied: "Not really. I was ultimately disappointed in the way that the film turned out." She explained that the screenplay was her attempt to answer the question that students most frequently asked her, "What's going to happen to Arnold?" Nonetheless, Gene Siskel gives the movie three stars because it has Arnold saved by the loving care of his grandfather who is able after a time to return Arnold to his family.

President Obama, in his speech to the parents of the victims at Newtown, Connecticut, **"Unconscionable Evil,"** reveals the power of his eloquent rhetoric; he spoke as a parent, confidentially, to parents who must somehow cope with what is any parent's greatest nightmare—the loss of a child. By beginning with the words of Paul to Corinthians, who had lost heart, Obama set the tone of his message and spoke as a Christian who knows that God is always aware of us—even in our most horrendous moments—even when we may not be aware of Him and mistakenly think that He is absent. Like Job, who never lost his trust in the God who-shows-up—even when he had lost everything (his children, his health, his status, and his wealth)—Obama recognizes (as Job learned) that there is no "answer" to the paradox of how God can be good and yet tolerate evil. We, like grown-up children, must trust Him as children who depend utterly on their parents and trust them unconditionally and absolutely. In short, "In the face of unconscionable evil," we must rely on our love for one another, and bear one another's burdens (Gal 6:2). Nevertheless, as good as Obama's eloquent and compassionate rhetoric is, his concluding statement that "God has called them all home" is bad theology. God did not call anyone home that day. A mad man sent them Home.

Criteria for Choosing Readings for Socratic Discussion

Vital to the success of the seminar is a careful selection of the readings which are, in the end, the real teachers. According to George Anastaplo of the Chicago Public Schools Socratic Seminar, "The ultimate leaders of the best seminar discussions are the authors of the best books. It is only in the best books that one is likely to encounter the finest examples of minds at work." Indeed, unless the readings are carefully chosen according to the tested and established criteria of the Great Books Foundation (Chicago, IL), there can be no hope of having successful meetings in which there is a mutual increase in understanding and enjoyment. In order of importance, here are four key criteria for choosing good selections.

1. **The readings must be able to support extensive reading and discussion.** The selections must yield multiple interpretations, that is, they must raise interpretive questions about an author's meaning that is not explicit. Only well-written works that are thematically complex and cohesive suggest real answers—that is, differing interpretations that can be supported with evidence from the text rather than merely being a matter of personal opinion. While every work of literature requires some degree of interpretation, not all works hold up under an extended analysis. This means that not all so-called "classics" qualify for a Socratic Seminar. In other words, if the meaning and intention of a book is transparent to the reader, it cannot sustain a genuine search for meaning because it cannot generate questions that have the vital element of doubt about their answers. For example, as appealing and uplifting as are novels like Wilson's *Where the Red Fern Grows* and Collier's *My Brother Sam is Dead*, they cannot function in Socratic discussion because they are too thin, their meaning obvious, and their intention transparent.
2. **The readings must evoke real questions for leaders as well as participants.** This second criterion is but the other side of the coin. Since leaders do not rely on a teacher's manual or refer to an answer key

in preparing for Socratic discussion, they must be able to write questions on a selection that are real questions *for them*—that is, questions that raise more than one legitimate answer (at least two) **or** that *seem* to have no answer at all (complete doubt). In other words, leaders do **not** write questions that they believe someone else may have doubt about. They write questions that *they* have doubt about. Because the leaders own questions reflect their personal curiosity about the meaning of a work, and because leaders never give their own personal opinions, participants begin to see their teacher(s) and peers in a new role—as active and involved partners in discussion, as co-learners and not as answer-givers.

3. **The readings must be reasonably self-contained.** The best kind of reading that illustrates this third criteria is the short story. In stories like Saroyan's "Gaston" or Cheever's "Reunion," the reader is given all the information needed to arrive at a good grasp of their overall theme(s). In other words, shorter works are more manageable in discussion and more suited to two readings and intensive analysis. In contrast, works that are not self-contained invite numerous questions that cannot be answered on the basis of the text alone and invite mere speculation where one answer begins to sound as plausible as another. The real problem with this criterion is longer works, full-length novels. But this obstacle can be overcome if the reading is carefully divided into chapters that are more or less self-contained. Sometimes the author makes this division for us. For example, Camus divides *The Stranger* into two clearly self-contained parts and *The Adventures of Huckleberry Finn* follows an episodic plot that can be easily divided for several discussions.
4. **The readings must be age and grade appropriate.** As Louise Rosenblatt (1968) reminds us in her seminal *Literature as Exploration*, reading is an active process, that is, a *transaction* between reader and the story that involves not merely "decoding" the text but, more importantly, a recognition of what the student brings to the text—his or her intellectual grasp, emotional maturity, and life experience. Recognition of these three key elements explains why student interpretations vary, why they ignore or overlook certain elements of the story, and why some interpretations are better (more comprehensive and defendable) than others.

Given this fourth criterion, consider the following examples: *Flowers for Algernon* would not be an appropriate reading for middle school but *Running Loose* or *The Giver* is. Similarly, *Sons and Lovers* by D.H. Lawrence would not be appropriate for high school but *Much Ado About Nothing* would be. Hemingway's "The Killers" (which has a fourth grade readability level) would not be appropriate for middle school but Richard Wilbur's "A Game of Catch," Shirley Jackson's "Charles," or Carson McCullers' "Sucker" would be well received. *Lady Chatterly's Lover* ought not be in a high school curriculum but Ibsen's *A Doll's House* always evokes strong reactions. *Antigone* is beyond the grasp of middle school students but not a western like *Shane*. *Anna Karenina* is too sophisticated for high school students but not Jane Austen's *Pride and Prejudice*.

In short, teachers must remember that

> in the selection of literary materials to be presented to students, it is **not** enough merely to think of what they **ought** to read. Choices must also reflect a sense of the possible links between the readings and the present level of a student's emotional maturity
>
> (Rosenblatt, third edition, 42)

The implication, then, is that "if the language, the setting, and the theme all are too alien, even a 'great work' [a classic] will fail. Books must be chosen that hold out some link with the student's past and present preoccupations, anxieties, and ambitions."

CHAPTER

10 Lesson Plans 7 and 8

How Important is a Girlfriend, a Brother, or a Parent in Your Life?

Lesson Plan 7: "Sucker," "Two Soldiers," and "Gaston"

1. **Focus:** Are you a bumper-sticker patriot? Complete the Exercise after Obama's speech on patriotism and compare your answers with your teacher and your classmates.
2. **Objective:** To review the Three Kinds of Questions and Qualities of Good Discussion Questions.
3. **Purpose:** To prepare students for small-group discussion.
4. **Input and modeling:** Plot-check Quiz on Three Kinds of Questions and Exercise on the Qualities of Good Questions on "Gaston" and "Two Soldiers."
5. **Checking for understanding:** Review the Plot-check Quiz and the Exercise Qualities of Good Questions.
6. **Guided Practice:** Discussion of two basic questions of interpretation.
7. **Closure:** Essay: each student's resolution of one of the basic questions.

Text: Carson McCullers (1987). "Sucker," *Collected Stories*. New York: Houghton Mifflin Co (pages 1–10).
William Faulkner (1950). "Two Soldiers," *Collected Stories of William Faulkner*. New York: Random House (pages 81–99).
William Saroyan (1962). "Gaston," *The Atlantic Monthly*. Published as a book in 1963.

Films:

- "Two Soldiers" video (The American Film Institute, 30 mins; Monterey home video, dir. Christopher Lula).
- "Two Soldiers" video (Shoe Picture Company, 40 mins; dir. Aaron Schneider. Academy Award 2005—Short Subject).

Sucker

Carson McCullers

It was always like I had a room to myself. Sucker slept in my bed with me but that didn't interfere with anything. The room was mine and I used it as I wanted to. Once I remember sawing a trap door in the floor. Last year when I was a sophomore in high school I tacked on my wall some pictures of girls from magazines and one of them was just in her underwear. My mother never bothered me because she had the younger kids to look after. And Sucker thought anything I did was always swell.

Whenever I would bring any of my friends back to my room all I had to do was just glance once at Sucker and he would get up from whatever he was busy with and maybe half smile at me, and leave without saying a word. He never brought kids back there. He's twelve, four years younger than I am, and he always knew without me even telling him that I didn't want kids that age meddling with my things.

Half the time I used to forget that Sucker isn't my brother. He's my first cousin but practically ever since I remember he's been in our family. You see his folks were killed in a wreck when he was a baby. To me and my kid sisters he was like our brother.

Sucker used to always remember and believe every word I said. That's how he got his nick-name. Once a couple of years ago I told him that if he'd jump off our garage with an umbrella it would act as a parachute and he wouldn't fall hard. He did it and busted his knee. That's just one instance. And the funny thing was that no matter how many times he got fooled he would still believe me. Not that he was dumb in other ways—it was just the way he acted with me. He would look at everything I did and quietly take it in.

There is one thing I have learned, but it makes me feel guilty and is hard to figure out. If a person admires you a lot you despise him and don't care—and it is the person who doesn't notice you that you are apt to admire. This is not easy to realize. Maybelle Watts, this senior at school, acted like she was the Queen of Sheba and even humiliated me. Yet at the same time I would have done anything in the world to get her attentions. All I could think about day and night was Maybelle until I was nearly crazy. When Sucker was a little kid and on up until the time I was twelve I guess I treated him as bad as Maybelle did me.

Now that Sucker has changed so much it is a little hard to remember him as he used to be. I never imagined anything would suddenly happen that would make us both VERY different. I never knew that in order to get what has happened straight in my mind I would want to think back on him as he used to be and compare and try to get things settled. If I could have seen ahead maybe I would have acted different.

I never noticed him much or thought about him and when you consider how long we have had the same room together it is funny the few things I remember. He used to talk to himself a lot when he'd think he was alone—all about him fighting gangsters and being on ranches and that sort of kids' stuff. He'd get in the bathroom and stay as long as an hour and sometimes his voice would go up high and excited and you could hear him all over the house. Usually, though, he was very quiet. He didn't have many boys in the neighborhood to buddy with and his face had the look of a kid who is watching a game and waiting to be asked to play. He didn't mind wearing the sweaters and coats that I outgrew, even if the sleeves did flop down too big and make his wrists look as thin and white as a little girl's. That is how I remember him—getting a little bigger every year but still being the same. That was Sucker up until a few months ago when all this trouble began.

Maybelle was somehow mixed up in what happened so I guess I ought to start with her. Until I knew her I hadn't given much time to girls. Last fall she sat next to me in General Science class and that was when I first began to notice her. Her hair is the brightest yellow I ever saw. And occasionally she would wear it set into curls with some sort of gluey stuff. Her fingernails are pointed and manicured and painted a shiny red. All during class I used to watch Maybelle, nearly all the time except when I thought she was going to look my way or when the teacher called on me. I couldn't keep my eyes off her hands, for one thing. They are very little and white except for that red stuff, and when she would turn the pages of her book she always licked her thumb and held out her little finger and turned very slowly. It is impossible to describe Maybelle. All the boys are crazy about her but she didn't even notice me. For one thing she's almost two years older than I am. Between periods I used to try and pass very close to her in the halls but she would hardly ever smile at me. All I could do was sit and look at her in class—and sometimes it was like the whole room could hear my heart beating and I waited to holler or light out and run for hell.

At night, in bed, I would imagine about Maybelle. Often this would keep me from sleeping until as late as one or two o'clock. Sometimes Sucker would wake up and ask me why I couldn't get settled and I'd tell him to hush his mouth. I suppose I was mean to him lots of times. I guess I wanted to ignore somebody like Maybelle did me. You could always tell by Sucker's face when his feelings were hurt. I don't remember all the ugly remarks I must have made because even when I was saying them my mind was on Maybelle.

That went on for nearly three months and then somehow she began to change. In the halls she would speak to me and every morning she copied my homework. At lunch time once I danced with her in the gym. One afternoon I got up nerve and went around to her house with a carton of cigarettes. I knew she smoked in the girls' basement and sometimes outside of school—and I didn't want to take her candy because I think that's been run into the ground. She was very nice and it seemed to me everything was going to change.

It was that night when this trouble really started. I had come into my room late and Sucker was already asleep. I felt too happy and keyed up to get in a comfortable position and I was awake thinking about Maybelle a long time. Then I dreamed about her and it seemed I kissed her. It was a surprise to wake up and see the dark. I lay still and a little while passed before I could come to and understand where I was. The house was quiet and it was a very dark night.

Sucker's voice was a shock to me.

"Pete? . . ."

I didn't answer anything or even move.

"You do like me as much as if I was your own brother, don't you Pete?"

I couldn't get over the surprise of everything until it was like this was the real dream instead of the other.

"You have liked me all the time like I was your own brother, haven't you?"

"Sure," I said.

Then I got up for a few minutes. It was cold and I was glad to come back to bed. Sucker hung on to my back. He felt little and warm and I could feel his warm breathing on my shoulder.

"No matter what you did I always knew you liked me."

I was wide awake and my mind seemed mixed up in a strange way. There was this happiness about Maybelle and all that—but at the same time something about Sucker and his voice when he said these things made me take notice. Anyway I guess you understand people better when you are happy than when something is worrying you. It was like I had never really thought about Sucker until then. I felt I had always been mean to him. One night a few weeks before I had heard him crying in the dark. He said he had lost a boy's beebee gun and was scared to let anybody know. He wanted me to tell him what to do. I was sleepy and tried to make him hush and when he wouldn't I kicked at him. That was just one of the things I remembered. It seemed to me he had always been a lonesome kid. I felt bad.

There is something about a dark cold night that makes you feel close to someone you're sleeping with. When you talk together it is like you are the only people awake in the town.

"You're a swell kid, Sucker," I said.

It seemed to me suddenly that I did like him more than anybody else I knew—more than any other boy, more than my sisters, more in a certain way even than Maybelle. I felt good all over and it was like when they play sad music in the movies. I wanted to show Sucker how much I really thought of him and make up for the way I'd always treated him. We talked for a good while that night. His voice was fast and it was like he had been saving up these things to tell me for a long time. He mentioned that he was going to try to build a canoe and that the kids down the block wouldn't let him in on their football team and I don't know what all. I talked some too and it was a good feeling to think of him taking in everything I said so seriously. I even spoke of Maybelle a little, only I made out like it was her who had been running after me all this time. He asked questions about high school and so forth. His voice was excited and he kept on talking fast like he could never get the words out in time. When I went to sleep he was still talking and I could still feel his breathing on my shoulder, warm and close.

During the next couple of weeks I saw a lot of Maybelle. She acted as though she really cared for me a little. Half the time I felt so good I hardly knew what to do with myself.

But I didn't forget about Sucker. There were a lot of old things in my bureau drawer I'd been saving—boxing gloves and Tom Swift books and second-rate fishing tackle. All this I turned over to him. We had some more talks together and it was really like I was knowing him for the first time. When there was a long cut on his cheek I knew he had been monkeying around with this new first razor set of mine, but I didn't say anything. His face seemed different now. He used to look timid and sort of like he was afraid of a whack over the head. That expression was gone. His face, with those wide-open eyes and his ears sticking out and his mouth never quite shut, had the look of a person who is surprised and expecting something swell.

Once I started to point him out to Maybelle and tell her he was my kid brother. It was an afternoon when a murder mystery was on at the movie. I had earned a dollar working for my dad and I gave Sucker a quarter to go and get candy and so forth. With the rest I took Maybelle. We were sitting near the back and I saw Sucker come in. He began to stare at the screen the minute he stepped past the ticket man and he stumbled down the aisle without noticing where he was going. I started to punch Maybelle but couldn't quite make up my mind. Sucker looked a little silly—walking like a drunk with his eyes glued to the movie. He was wiping his reading glasses on his shirttail and his knickers flopped down. He went on until he got to the first few rows where the kids usually sit. I never did punch Maybelle. But I got to thinking it was good to have both of them at the movie with the money I earned.

I guess things went on like this for about a month or six weeks. I felt so good I couldn't settle down to study or put my mind on anything. I wanted to be friendly with everybody. There were times when I just had to talk to some person. And usually that would be Sucker. He felt as good as I did. Once he said: "Pete, I am gladder that you are like my brother than anything else in the world."

Then something happened between Maybelle and me. I never have figured out just what it was. Girls like her are hard to understand. She began to act different toward me. At first I wouldn't let myself believe this and tried to think it was just my imagination. She didn't act glad to see me anymore. Often she went out riding with this fellow on the football team who owns this yellow roadster. The car was the color of her hair and after school she would ride off with him, laughing and looking into his face. I couldn't think of anything to do about it and she was on my mind all day and night. When I did get a chance to go out with her she was snippy and didn't seem to notice me. This made me feel like something was the matter—I would worry about my shoes clopping too loud on the floor, or the fly of my pants, or the bumps on my chin. Sometimes when Maybelle was around, a devil would get into me and I'd hold my face stiff and call grown men by their last names without the Mister and say rough things. In the night I would wonder what made me do all this until I was too tired for sleep.

At first I was so worried I just forgot about Sucker. Then later he began to get on my nerves. He was always hanging around until I would get back from high school, always looking like he had something to say to me or wanted me to tell him. He made me a magazine rack in his Manual Training class and one week he saved his lunch money and bought me three packs of cigarettes. He couldn't seem to take it in that I had things on my mind and didn't want to fool with him. Every afternoon it would be the same—him in my room with this waiting expression on his face. Then I wouldn't say anything or I'd maybe answer him rough-like and he would finally go on out.

I can't divide that time up and say this happened one day and that the next. For one thing I was so mixed up the weeks just slid along into each other and I felt like hell and didn't care. Nothing definite was said or done. Maybelle still rode around with this fellow in his yellow roadster and sometimes she would smile at me and sometimes not. Every afternoon I went from one place to another where I thought she would be. Either she would act almost nice and I would begin thinking how things would finally clear up and she would care for me—or else she'd behave so that if she hadn't been a girl I'd have wanted to grab her by that white little neck and choke her. The more ashamed I felt for making a fool of myself the more I ran after her.

Sucker kept getting on my nerves more and more. He would look at me as though he sort of blamed me for something, but at the same time knew that it wouldn't last long. He was growing fast and for some reason began to stutter when he talked. Sometimes he had nightmares or would throw up his breakfast. Mom got him a bottle of cod liver oil.

Then the finish came between Maybelle and me. I met her going to the drug store and asked for a date. When she said no I remarked something sarcastic. She told me she was sick and tired of my being around and that she had never cared a rap about me. She said all that. I just stood there and didn't answer anything. I walked home very slowly.

For several afternoons I stayed in my room by myself. I didn't want to go anywhere or talk to anyone. When Sucker would come in and look at me sort of funny I'd yell at him to get out. I didn't want to think of Maybelle and I sat at my desk reading *Popular Mechanics* or whittling at a toothbrush rack I was making. It seemed to me I was putting that girl out of my mind pretty well.

But you can't help what happens to you at night. That is what made things how they are now.

You see a few nights after Maybelle said those words to me I dreamed about her again. It was like that first time and I was squeezing Sucker's arm so tight I woke him up. He reached for my hand.

"Pete, what's the matter with you?"

All of a sudden I felt so mad my throat choked—at myself and the dream and Maybelle and Sucker and every single person I knew. I remembered all the times Maybelle had humiliated me and everything bad that had ever happened. It seemed to me for a second that nobody would ever like me but a sap like Sucker.

"Why is it we aren't buddies like we were before? Why—?"

"Shut your damn trap!" I threw off the cover and got up and turned on the light. He sat in the middle of the bed, his eyes blinking and scared.

There was something in me and I couldn't help myself. I don't think anybody ever gets that mad but once. Words came without me knowing what they would be. It was only afterward that I could remember each thing I said and see it all in a clear way.

"Why aren't we buddies? Because you're the dumbest slob I ever saw! Nobody cares anything about you! And just because I felt sorry for you sometimes and tried to act decent don't think I give a damn about a dumb-bunny like you!"

If I talked loud or hit him it wouldn't have been so bad. But my voice was slow and like I was very calm. Sucker's mouth was partway open and he looked as though he'd knocked his funny bone. His face was white and sweat came out on his forehead. He wiped it away with the back of his hand and for a minute his arm stayed raised that way as though he was holding something away from him.

"Don't you know a single thing? Haven't you ever been around at all? Why don't you get a girl friend instead of me? What kind of sissy do you want to grow up to be anyway?"

I didn't know what was coming next. I couldn't help myself or think.

Sucker didn't move. He had on one of my pajama jackets and his neck stuck out skinny and small. His hair was damp on his forehead.

"Why do you always hang around me? Don't you know when you're not wanted?"

Afterward I could remember the change In Sucker's face. Slowly that blank look went away and he closed his mouth. His eyes got narrow and his fists shut. There had never been such a look on him before. It was like every second he was getting older. There was a hard look to his eyes you don't see usually in a kid. A drop of sweat rolled down his chin and he didn't notice. He just sat there with those eyes on me and he didn't speak and his face was hard and didn't move.

"No you don't know when you're not wanted. You're too dumb. Just like your name—a dumb Sucker."

It was like something had busted inside me. I turned off the light and sat down in the chair by the window. My legs were shaking and I was so tired I could have bawled. The room was cold and dark. I sat there for a long time and smoked a squashed cigarette I had saved. Outside the yard was black and quiet. After a while I heard Sucker lie down.

I wasn't mad any more, only tired. It seemed awful to me that I had talked like that to a kid only twelve. I couldn't take it all in. I told myself I would go over to him and try to make it up. But I just sat there in the cold until a long time had passed. I planned how I could straighten it out in the morning. Then, trying not to squeak the springs, I got back in bed.

Sucker was gone when I woke up the next day. And later when I wanted to apologize as I had planned he looked at me in this new hard way so that I couldn't say a word.

All of that was two or three months ago. Since then Sucker has grown faster than any boy I ever saw. He's almost as tall as I am and his bones have gotten heavier and bigger. He won't wear any of my old clothes anymore and has bought his first pair of long pants—with some leather suspenders to hold them up. Those are just the changes that are easy to see and put into words.

Our room isn't mine at all anymore. He's gotten up this gang of kids and they have a club. When they aren't digging trenches in some vacant lot and fighting they are always in my room. On the door there is some foolishness written in Mercurochrome saying "Woe to the Outsider who Enters" and signed with crossed bones and their secret initials. They have rigged up a radio and every afternoon it blares out music. Once as I was coming in I heard a boy telling something in a low voice about what he saw in the back of his big brother's automobile. I could guess what I didn't hear. That's what her and my brother do. It's the truth—parked in the car. For a minute Sucker looked surprised and his face was almost like it used to be. Then he got hard and tough again. "Sure, dumbbell. We know all that." They didn't notice me. Sucker began telling them how in two years he was planning to be a trapper in Alaska.

But most of the time Sucker stays by himself. It is worse when we are alone together in the room. He sprawls across the bed in those long corduroy pants with the suspenders and just stares at me with that hard, half-sneering look. I fiddle around my desk and can't get settled because of those eyes of his. And the thing is I just have to study because I've gotten three bad cards this term already. If I flunk English I can't graduate next year. I don't want to be a bum and I just have to get my mind on it. I don't care a flip for Maybelle or any particular girl anymore and it's only this thing between Sucker and me that is the trouble now. We never speak except when we have to before the family. I don't even want to call him Sucker anymore and unless I forget I call him by his real name, Richard. At night I can't study with him in the room and I have to hang around the drug store, smoking and doing nothing, with the fellows who loaf there.

More than anything I want to be easy in my mind again. And I miss the way Sucker and I were for a while in a funny, sad way that before this I never would have believed. But everything is so different that there seems to be nothing I can do to get it right. I've sometimes thought if we could have it out in a big fight that would help. But I can't fight him because he's four years younger. And another thing—sometimes this look in his eyes makes me almost believe that if Sucker could he would kill me.

"Sucker"

PLOT-CHECK QUIZ

Directions: On your own paper or in the space beneath, answer each question briefly, and then identify the type of each question: print FACT for factual, INT for interpretation, and EVAL for evaluation.

1. What are Pete and Sucker's ages and how are they related?

2. What is the "trouble" that Pete talks about in the opening of the story?

3. How is Maybelle Watts somehow mixed up in the trouble between Pete and Sucker?

4. What does Pete tell Sucker about his relationship with Maybelle?

5. How does Maybelle dump Pete?

6. How does Pete react to Maybelle's rejection?

7. How does Pete dump Sucker?

8. Why was Sucker so hurt by the way that Pete told him off?

9. How does Sucker react to Pete's rejection?

10. What explanation does Pete give for not apologizing to Sucker?

"Sucker"

REVIEW QUIZ ON QUALITIES OF GOOD DISCUSSION QUESTIONS

Directions: On your own paper, mark GOOD if a question would lead to a disagreement based on the story. If the question lacks one of the needed qualities, mark it:

NC if the question is NOT CLEAR and would have to be explained.
NS if the question is NOT SPECIFIC and could be asked of any story.
LD for LACKS DOUBT since it cannot be answered in more than one way.
FACT for FACTUAL and cannot be discussed.
EVAL for EVALUATION and not about understanding the story.

1. What kind of relationship is there between Pete and Sucker?

2. What's the connection between Pete, Sucker, and Maybelle?

3. Why does Sucker think that Pete doesn't like him anymore?

4. What's wrong with Sucker?

5. Why does Sucker do everything Pete tells him even though he isn't stupid?

6. Do you ever dream about things that you are worried about?

7. Was Pete out of it?

8. Why is Pete so upset about telling off Sucker?

9. What is the meaning of the title?

10. Does Pete feel bad about hurting Sucker's feelings?

11. Why does Pete change his mind about introducing Maybelle to Sucker?

12. Is Pete's problem as big as Sucker's problem?

13. Should Pete have gotten help when he didn't know how to make up with Sucker?

14. Does Pete feel like a fool for having tried to get Maybelle's attention?

15. In this story is Pete looking for a way to be friends again with Sucker or is he trying to excuse his meanness?

Socratic Seminar

Does Pete look back on his relationship with Sucker to find a way to become friends again or to excuse his own actions towards Sucker?

If he wants to be friends again, then:

1. Why does Pete qualify so many statements with "I guess" or "I suppose" or "maybe would have acted differently"?
2. Does Pete use Maybelle's rejection of him to excuse his rejection of Sucker?
3. Is Pete excusing himself when he says what happened at night made things how they are between himself and Sucker?
4. Why does Pete say he couldn't help himself when he told off Sucker?
5. Are we to believe it IS Sucker's fault that Pete cannot apologize to Sucker?

If he is trying to rationalize his conduct, then:

6. Why does Pete admit that he feels guilty that people tend to despise those who admire them a lot?
7. Is Pete sincere when he says he did like Sucker "more than anybody else"?
8. Why does Pete recognize he hurt Sucker so much more because his voice was slow and calm when he told off Sucker?
9. Why does it still bother Pete so much that he can do nothing to get his relationship with Sucker restored?
10. Why is Pete still uneasy in his mind three months after his breakup with Sucker?

Lesson Plan 8: "Two Soldiers"

1. Focus:	Journal: What is your definition of patriotism? What is the difference between a genuine and a phony patriot?
2. Objective:	To review the Three Kinds of Questions and Qualities of Good Discussion Questions.
3. Purpose:	To prepare students for small-group discussion.
4. Input and Modeling:	Plot-check Quiz on Three Kinds of Questions and Exercise on the Qualities of Good Questions on the short story by William Faulkner.

5. Checking for Understanding:	Review the Plot-check Quiz and the Exercise on Qualities of Good Questions.
6. Guided Practice:	Discussion of two basic questions of interpretation.
7. Closure:	An essay on each individual's resolution of one of the basic questions just discussed.
Text:	William Faulkner, *Collected Stories of William Faulkner* (1950, New York: Random House, "Two Soldiers" (pp. 81–99).
Films:	○ *Two Soldiers* video (The American Film Institute, 30 mins; Monterey home video, dir. Christopher Lula). ○ *Two Soldiers* video (Shoe Picture Company, 40 mins; dir. Aaron Schneider. Academy Award 2005—Short Subject).

Two Soldiers

William Faulkner

ME AND PETE would go down to Old Man Killegrew's and listen to his radio. We would wait until after supper, after dark, and we would stand outside Old Man Killegrew's parlor window, and we could hear it because Old Man Killegrew's wife was deaf, and so he run the radio as loud as it would run, and so me and Pete could hear it plain as Old Man Killegrew's wife could, I reckon, even standing outside with the window closed.

And that night I said, "What? Japanese? What's a pearl harbor?" and Pete said, "Hush."

And so we stood there, it was cold, listening to the fellow in the radio talking, only I couldn't make no heads nor tails neither out of it. Then the fellow said that would be all for a while, and me and Pete walked back up the road to home, and Pete told me what it was. Because he was nigh twenty and he had done finished the Consolidated last June and he knowed a heap: about them Japanese dropping bombs on Pearl Harbor and that Pearl Harbor was across the water.

"Across what water?" I said. "Across that Government reservoy up at Oxford?"

"Naw," Pete said. "Across the big water. The Pacific Ocean."

We went home. Maw and pap was already asleep, and me and Pete laid in the bed, and I still couldn't understand where it was, and Pete told me again the Pacific Ocean.

"What's the matter with you?" Pete said. "You're going on nine years old. You been in school now ever since September. Ain't you learned nothing yet?"

"I reckon we ain't got as fer as the Pacific Ocean yet," I said.

We was still sowing the vetch then that ought to been all finished by the fifteenth of November, because pap was still behind, just like he had been ever since me and Pete had knowed him. And we had firewood to git in, too, but every night me and Pete would go down to Old Man Killegrew's and stand outside his parlor window in the cold and listen to his radio; then we would come back home and lay in the bed and Pete would tell me what it was. That is, he would tell me for a while. Then he wouldn't tell me. It was like he didn't want to talk about it no more. He would tell me to shut up because he wanted to go to sleep, but he never wanted to go to sleep.

He would lay there, a heap stiller than if he was asleep, and it would be something, I could feel it coming out of him, like he was mad at me even, only I knowed he wasn't thinking about me, or like he was worried about something, and it wasn't that neither, because he never had nothing to worry about. He never got behind like pap, let alone stayed behind.

Pap give him ten acres when he graduated from the Consolidated, and me and Pete both reckoned pap was durn glad to get shut of at least ten acres, less to have to worry with himself; and Pete had them ten acres all sowed to vetch and busted out and bedded for the winter, and so it wasn't that.

But it was something. And still we would go down to Old Man Killegrew's every night and listen to his radio, and they was at it in the Philippines now, but General MacArthur was holding um. Then we would come back home and lay in the bed, and Pete wouldn't tell me nothing or talk at all. He would just lay there still as a ambush and when I would touch him, his side or his leg would feel hard and still as iron, until after a while I would go to sleep.

Then one night it was the first time he had said nothing to me except to jump on me about not chopping enough wood at the wood tree where we was cutting he said, "I got to go."

"Go where?" I said.

"To that war," Pete said.

"Before we even finish gettin' in the firewood?"

"Firewood, hell," Pete said.

"All right," I said. "When we going to start?"

But he wasn't even listening. He laid there, hard and still as iron in the dark. "I got to go," he said. "I jest ain't going to put up with no folks treating the Unity States that way."

"Yes," I said. "Firewood or no firewood, I reckon we got to go."

This time he heard me. He laid still again, but it was a different kind of still.

"You?" he said. "To a war?"

"You'll whup the big uns and I'll whup the little uns," I said.

Then he told me I couldn't go. At first I thought he just never wanted me tagging after him, like he wouldn't leave me go with him when he went sparking them girls of Tull's.

Then he told me the Army wouldn't leave me go because I was too little, and then I knowed he really meant it and that I couldn't go nohow noways. And somehow I hadn't believed until then that he was going himself, but now I knowed he was and that he wasn't going to leave me go with him a-tall.

"I'll chop the wood and tote the water for you-all then!" I said. "You got to have wood and water!" Anyway, he was listening to me now. He wasn't like iron now. He turned onto his side and put his hand on my chest because it was me that was laying straight and hard on my back now. "No," he said. "You got to stay here and help pap."

"Help him what?" I said. "He ain't never caught up nohow. He can't get no further behind. He can sholy take care of this little shirttail of a farm while me and you are whupping them Japanese. I got to go too. If you got to go, then so have I."

"No," Pete said. "Hush now. Hush." And he meant it, and I knowed he did. Only I made sho from his own mouth. I quit.

"So I just can't go then," I said.

"No," Pete said. "You just can't go. You're too little, in the first place, and in the second place "

"All right," I said. "Then shut up and leave me go to sleep." So he hushed then and laid back. And I laid there like I was already asleep, and pretty soon he was asleep and I knowed it was the wanting to go to the war that had worried him and kept him awake, and now that he had decided to go, he wasn't worried any more.

The next morning he told maw and pap. Maw was all right. She cried.

"No," she said, crying, "I don't want him to go. I would rather go myself in his place, if I could. I don't want to save the country. Them Japanese could take it and keep it, so long as they left me and my family and my children alone. But I remember my brother Marsh in that other war. He had to go to that one when he wasn't but nineteen, and our mother couldn't understand it then any more than I can now. But she told Marsh if he had to go, he had to go. And so, if Pete's got to go to this one, he's got to go to it. Jest don't ask me to understand why."

But pap was the one. He was the feller. "To the war?" he said. "Why, I just don't see a bit of use in that. You ain't old enough for the draft, and the country ain't being invaded. Our President in Washington, D. C. is watching the conditions and he will notify us. Besides, in that other war your ma just mentioned, I was drafted and sent clean to Texas and was held there nigh eight months until they finally quit fighting. It seems to me that that, along with your Uncle Marsh who received a actual wound on the battlefields of France, is enough for me and mine to have to do to protect the country, at least in my lifetime. Besides, what'll I do for help on the farm with you gone? It seems to me I'll get mighty far behind."

"You been behind as long as I can remember," Pete said. "Anyway, I'm going. I got to."

"Of course he's got to go," I said. "Them Japanese"

"You hush your mouth!" maw said, crying. "Nobody's talking to you! Go and get me a armful of wood! That's what you can do!"

So I got the wood. And all the next day, while me and Pete and pap was getting in as much wood as we could in that time because Pete said how pap's idea of plenty of wood was one more stick laying against the wall that maw ain't put on the fire yet, Maw was getting Pete ready to go. She washed and mended his clothes and cooked him a shoe box of vittles. And that night me and Pete laid in the bed and listened to her packing his grip and crying, until after a while Pete got up in his nightshirt and went back there, and I could hear them talking, until at last maw said, "You got to go, and so I want you to go. But I don't understand it, and I won't never, and so don't expect me to." And Pete come back and got into the bed again and laid again still and hard as iron on his back, and then he said, and he wasn't talking to me, he wasn't talking to nobody: "I got to go. I just got to."

"Sho you got to," I said. "Them Japanese." He turned over hard, he kind of surged over onto his side, looking at me in the dark.

"Anyway, you're all right," he said. "I expected to have more trouble with you than with all the rest of them put together."

"I reckon I can't help it neither," I said. "But maybe it will run a few years longer and I can get there. Maybe someday I will jest walk in on you."

"I hope not," Pete said. "Folks don't go to wars for fun. A man don't leave his maw crying just for fun."

"Then why are you going?" I said.

"I got to," he said. "I just got to. Now you go on to sleep. I got to ketch that early bus in the morning."

"All right," I said. "I hear tell Memphis is a big place. How will you find where the Army's at?"

"I'll ask somebody where to go to join it," Pete said. "Go on to sleep now."

"Is that what you'll ask for? Where to join the Army?" I said.

"Yes," Pete said. He turned onto his back again. "Shut up and go to sleep."

We went to sleep. The next morning we et breakfast by lamplight because the bus would pass at six o'clock. Maw wasn't crying now. She jest looked grim and busy, putting breakfast on the table while we et it. Then she finished packing Pete's grip, except he never wanted to take no grip to the war, but maw said decent folks never went nowhere, not even to a war, without a change of clothes and something to tote them in. She put in the shoe box of fried chicken and biscuits and she put the Bible in, too, and then it was time to go. We didn't know until then that maw wasn't going to the bus. She jest brought Pete's cap and overcoat, and still she didn't cry no more, she jest stood with her hands on Pete's shoulders and she didn't move, but somehow, and just holding Pete's shoulders, she looked as hard and fierce as when Pete had turned toward me in the bed last night and tole me that anyway I was all right.

"They could take the country and keep the country, so long as they never bothered me and mine," she said. Then she said, "Don't never forget who you are. You ain't rich and the rest of the world outside of Frenchman's Bend never heard of you. But your blood is good as any blood anywhere, and don't you never forget it."

Then she kissed him, and then we was out of the house, with pap toting Pete's grip whether Pete wanted him to or not. There wasn't no dawn even yet, not even after we had stood on the highway by the mailbox, a while. Then we seen the lights of the bus coming and I was watching the bus until it come up and Pete flagged it, and then, sho enough, there was daylight: it had started while I wasn't watching. And now me and Pete expected pap to say something else foolish, like he done before, about how Uncle Marsh getting wounded in France and that trip to Texas pap taken in 1918 ought to be enough to save the Unity States in 1942, but he never. He done all right too. He jest said, "Good-by, son. Always remember what your ma told you and write her whenever you find the time." Then he shaken Pete's hand, and Pete looked at me a minute and put his hand on my head and rubbed my head durn nigh hard enough to wring my neck off and jumped into the bus, and the feller wound the door shut and the bus began to hum; then it was moving, humming and grinding and whining louder and louder; it was going fast, with two little red lights behind it that never seemed to get no littler, but just seemed to be running together until pretty soon they would touch and jest be one light. But they never did, and then the bus was gone, and even like it was, I could have pretty nigh busted out crying, nigh to nine years old and all.

Me and pap went back to the house. All that day we worked at the wood tree, and so I never had no good chance until about middle of the afternoon. Then I taken my slingshot and I would have liked to took all my bird eggs, too, because Pete had give me his collection and he holp me with mine, and he would like to git the box out and look at them as good as I would, even if he was nigh twenty years old.

But the box was too big to tote a long ways and have to worry with, so I just taken the shikepoke egg, because it was the best un, and wropped it up good into a matchbox and hid it and the slingshot under the corner of the barn. Then we et supper and went to bed, and I thought then how if I would 'a' had to stayed in that room and that bed like that even for one more night, I jest couldn't 'a' stood it. Then I could hear pap snoring, but I never heard no sound from maw, whether she was asleep or not, and I don't reckon she was. So I taken my shoes and drapped them out the window, and then I clumb out like I used to watch Pete do when he was still jest seventeen and pap held that he was too young yet to be tomcatting around at night, and wouldn't leave him out, and I put on my shoes and went to the barn and got the slingshot and the shikepoke egg and went to the highway.

It wasn't cold, it was jest durn confounded dark, and that highway stretched on in front of me like, without nobody using it, it had stretched out half again as fer just like a man does when he lays down, so that for a time it looked like full sun was going to ketch me before I had finished them twenty-two miles to Jefferson. But it didn't. Daybreak was jest starting when I walked up the hill into town. I could smell breakfast cooking in the cabins and I wished I had thought to brought me a cold biscuit, but that was too late now. And Pete had told me Memphis was a piece beyond Jefferson, but I never knowed it was no eighty miles. So I stood there on that empty square, with daylight coming and coming and the street lights still burning and that Law looking down at me, and me still eighty miles from Memphis, and it had took me all night to walk jest twenty-two miles, and so, by the time I got to Memphis at that rate, Pete would 'a' done already started for Pearl Harbor.

"Where do you come from?" the Law said.

And I told him again. "I got to get to Memphis. My brother's there."

You mean you ain't got any folks around here?" the Law said. "Nobody but that brother? What are you doing way off down here and your brother in Memphis?"

And I told him again, "I got to get to Memphis. I ain't got no time to waste talking about it and I ain't got time to walk it. I got to git there today."

"Come on here," the Law said.

We went down another street. And there was the bus, just like when Pete got into it yestiddy morning, except there wasn't no lights on it now and it was empty. There was a regular bus dee-po like a railroad dee-po, with a ticket counter and a feller behind it, and the Law said, "Set down over there," and I set down on the bench, and the Law said, "I want to use your telephone," and he talked in the telephone a minute and put it down and said to the feller behind the ticket counter, "Keep your eye on him. I'll be back as soon as Mrs. Habersham can arrange to get herself up and dressed." He went out. I got up and went to the ticket counter.

"I want to go to Memphis," I said.

"You bet," the feller said. "You set down on the bench now. Mr. Foote will be back in a minute."

"I don't know no Mr. Foote," I said. "I want to ride that bus to Memphis."

"You got some money?" he said. "It'll cost you seventy-two cents."

I taken out the matchbox and unwropped the shikepoke egg. "I'll swap you this for a ticket to Memphis," I said.

"What's that?" he said.

"It's a shikepoke egg," I said. "You never seen one before. It's worth a dollar. I'll take seventy-two cents fer it."

"No," he said, "the fellers that own that bus insist on a cash basis. If I started swapping tickets for bird eggs and livestock and such, they would fire me. You go and set down on the bench now, like Mr. Foote ..."

I started for the door, but he caught me, he put one hand on the ticket counter and jumped over it and caught up with me and reached his hand out to ketch my shirt. I whupped out my pocket-knife and snapped it open.

"You put a hand on me and I'll cut it off," I said.

I tried to dodge him and run at the door, but he could move quicker than any grown man I ever see, quick as Pete almost. He cut me off and stood with his back against the door and one foot raised a little, and there wasn't no other way to get out. "Get back on that bench and stay there," he said.

And there wasn't no other way out. And he stood there with his back against the door. So I went back to the bench. And then it seemed like to me that dee-po was full of folks.

There was that Law again, and there was two ladies in fur coats and their faces already painted. But they still looked like they had got up in a hurry and they still never liked it, a old one and a young one, looking down at me.

"He hasn't got a overcoat!" the old one said. "How in the world did he ever get down here by himself?"

"I ask you," the Law said. "I couldn't get nothing out of him except his brother is in Memphis and he wants to get back up there."

"That's right," I said. "I got to git to Memphis today."

"Of course you must," the old one said. "Are you sure you can find your brother when you get to Memphis?"

"I reckon I can," I said. "I ain't got but one and I have knowed him all my life. I reckon I will know him again when I see him."

The old one looked at me. "Somehow he doesn't look like he lives in Memphis," she said.

"He probably don't," the Law said. "You can't tell though. He might live anywhere, overhalls or not. This day and time they get scattered overnight from he hope to breakfast; boys and girls, too, almost before they can walk good. He might have been in Missouri or Texas either yestiddy, for all we know. But he don't seem to have any doubt his brother is in Memphis. All I know to do is send him up there and leave him look."

"Yes," the old one said.

The young one set down on the bench by me and opened a hand satchel and taken out a artermatic writing pen and some papers.

"Now, honey," the old one said, "we're going to see that you find your brother, but we must have a case history for our files first. We want to know your name and your brother's name and where you were born and when your parents died."

"I don't need no case history neither," I said. "All I want is to get to Memphis. I got to get there today."

"You see?" the Law said. He said it almost like he enjoyed it. "That's what I told you."

"You're lucky, at that, Mrs. Habersham," the bus feller said. "I don't think he's got a gun on him, but he can open that knife I mean, fast enough to suit any man." But the old one just stood there looking at me. "Well," she said. "Well. I really don't know what to do."

"I do," the bus feller said. "I'm going to give him a ticket out of my own pocket, as a measure of protecting the company against riot and bloodshed. And when Mr. Foote tells the city board about it, it will be a civic matter and they will not only reimburse me, they will give me a medal too. Hey, Mr. Foote?"

But never nobody paid him no mind. The old one still stood looking down at me. She said "Well," again. Then she taken a dollar from her purse and give it to the bus feller.

"I suppose he will travel on a child's ticket, won't he?"

"Wellum," the bus feller said, "I just don't know what the regulations would be. Likely I will be fired for not crating him and marking the crate Poison. But I'll risk it."

Then they were gone. Then the Law come back with a sandwich and give it to me.

"You're sure you can find that brother?" he said.

"I ain't yet convinced why not," I said. "If I don't see Pete first, he'll see me. He knows me too."

Then the Law went out for good, too, and I et the sandwich. Then more folks come in and bought tickets, and then the bus feller said it was time to go, and I got into the bus just like Pete done, and we was gone. I seen all the towns. I seen all of them. When the bus got to going good, I found out I was jest about wore out for sleep.

But there was too much I hadn't never saw before. We run out of Jefferson and run past fields and woods, then we would run into another town and out of that un and past fields and woods again, and then into another town with stores and gins and water tanks, and we run along by the railroad for a spell and I seen the signal arm move, and then I seen the train and then some more towns, and I was jest about plumb wore out for sleep, but I couldn't resk it. Then Memphis begun. It seemed like, to me, it went on for miles.

We would pass a patch of stores and I would think that was sholy it and the bus would even stop. But it wouldn't be Memphis yet and we would go on again past water tanks and smokestacks on top of the mills, and if they was gins and sawmills, I never knowed there was that many and I never seen any that big, and where they got enough cotton and logs to run um I don't know.

Then I see Memphis. I knowed I was right this time. It was standing up into the air. It looked like about a dozen whole towns bigger than Jefferson was set up on one edge in a field, standing up into the air higher than ara hill in all Yoknapatawpha County. Then we was in it, with the bus stopping ever' few feet, it seemed like to me, and cars rushing past on both sides of it and the street crowded with folks from ever'where in town that day, until I didn't see how there could 'a' been nobody left in Mis'sippi a-tall to even sell me a bus ticket, let alone write out no case histories.

Then the bus stopped. It was another bus dee-po, a heap bigger than the one in Jefferson. And I said, "All right. Where do folks join the Army?"

"What?" the bus feller said.

And I said it again, "Where do folks join the Army?"

"Oh," he said. Then he told me how to get there. I was afraid at first I wouldn't ketch on how to do in a town big as Memphis. But I caught on all right. I never had to ask but twice more. Then I was there, and I was durn glad to git out of all them rushing cars and shoving folks and all that racket for a spell, and I thought, It won't be long now, and I thought how if there was any kind of a crowd there that had done already joined the Army, too, Pete would likely see me before I seen him. And so I walked into the room. And Pete wasn't there.

He wasn't even there. There was a soldier with a big arrer head on his sleeve, writing, and two fellers standing in front of him, and there was some more folks there, I reckon. It seems to me I remember some more folks there. I went to the table where the soldier was writing, and I said,

"Where's Pete?" and he looked up and I said, "My brother. Pete Grier. Where is he?"

"What?" the soldier said. "Who?"

And I told him again. "He joined the Army yestiddy. He's going to Pearl Harbor. So am I. I want to ketch him. Where you all got him?" Now they were all looking at me, but I never paid them no mind. "Come on," I said. "Where is he?"

The soldier had quit writing. He had both hands spraddled out on the table. "Oh," he said.

"You're going, too, hah?"

"Yes," I said. "They got to have wood and water. I can chop it and tote it. Come on. Where's Pete?"

The soldier stood up. "Who let you in here?" he said. "Go on. Beat it."

"Durn that," I said. "You tell me where Pete ..."

I be dog if he couldn't move faster than the bus feller even. He never come over the table, he come around it, he was on me almost before I knowed it, so that I jest had time to jump back and whup out my pocket-knife and snap it open and hit one lick, and he hollered and jumped back and grabbed one hand with the other and stood there cussing and hollering.

One of the other fellers grabbed me from behind, and I hit at him with the knife, but I couldn't reach him. Then both of the fellers had me from behind, and then another soldier come out of a door at the back. He had on a belt with a britching strop over one shoulder.

"What the hell is this?" he said.

"That little son cut me with a knife!" the first soldier hollered. When he said that I tried to get at him again. but both them fellers was holding me, two against one, and the soldier with the backing strop said, "Here, here. Put your knife up, feller. None of us are armed. A man don't knife fight folks that are barehanded." I could begin to hear him then. He sounded jest like Pete talked to me. "Let him go," he said. They let me go. "Now what's all the trouble about?"

And I told him. "I see," he said. "And you come up to see if he was all right before he left."

"No," I said. "I came to ..."

But he had already turned to where the first soldier was wrapping a handkerchief around his hand.

"Have you got him?" he said. The first soldier went back to the table and looked at some papers.

"Here he is," he said. "He enlisted yestiddy. He's in a detachment leaving this morning for Little Rock." He had a watch stropped on his arm. He looked at it. "The train leaves in about fifty minutes. If I know country boys, they're probably all down there at the station right now."

"Get him up here," the one with the backing strop said. "Phone the station. Tell the porter to get him a cab. And you come with me," he said.

It was another office behind that un, with jest a table and some chairs. We set there while the soldier smoked, and it wasn't long; I knowed Pete's feet soon as I heard them. Then the first soldier opened the door and Pete come in. He never had no soldier clothes on. He looked jest like he did when he got on the bus yestiddy morning, except it seemed to me like it was at least a week, so much had happened, and I had done had to do so much traveling. He come in and there he was, looking at me like he hadn't never left home, except that here we was in Memphis, on the way to Pearl Harbor.

"What in durnation are you doing here?" he said.

And I told him, "You got to have wood and water to cook with. I can chop it and tote it for you-all."

"No," Pete said. "You're going back home."

"No, Pete," I said. "I got to go too. I got to. It hurts my heart, Pete."

"No," Pete said. He looked at the soldier. "I jest don't know what could have happened to him, lootenant," he said. "He never drawed a knife on anybody before in his life."

He looked at me. "What did you do it for?"

"I don't know," I said. "I jest had to. I jest had to git here. I jest had to find you."

"Well, don't you never do it again, you hear?" Pete said.

"You put that knife in your pocket and you keep it there. If I ever again hear of you drawing it on anybody, I'm coming back from wherever I am at and whup the fire out of you. You hear me?"

"I would pure cut a throat if it would bring you back to stay," I said. "Pete," I said. "Pete."

"No," Pete said. Now his voice wasn't hard and quick no more, it was almost quiet, and I knowed now I wouldn't never change him. "You must go home. You must look after maw, and I am depending on you to look after my ten acres. I want you to go back home. Today. Do you hear?"

"I hear," I said.

"Can he get back home by himself?" the soldier said.

"He come up here by himself," Pete said.

"I can get back, I reckon," I said. "I don't live in but one place. I don't reckon it's moved."

Pete taken a dollar out of his pocket and give it to me.

"That'll buy your bus ticket right to our mailbox," he said.

"I want you to mind the lootenant. He'll send you to the bus. And you go back home and you take care of maw and look after my ten acres and keep that durn knife in your pocket. You hear me?"

"Yes, Pete," I said.

"All right," Pete said. "Now I got to go." He put his hand on my head again. But this time he never wrung my neck.

He just laid his hand on my head a minute. And then I be dog if he didn't lean down and kiss me, and I heard his feet and then the door, and I never looked up and that was all, me setting there, rubbing the place where Pete kissed me and the soldier throwed back in his chair, looking out the window and coughing. He reached into his pocket and handed something to me without looking around. It was a piece of chewing gum.

"Much obliged," I said. "Well, I reckon I might as well start back. I got a right fer piece to go."

"Wait," the soldier said. Then he telephoned again and I said again I better start back, and he said again, "Wait. Remember what Pete told you."

So we waited, and then another lady come in, old, too, in a fur coat, too, but she smelled all right, she never had no artermatic writing pen nor no case history neither. She come in and the soldier got up, and she looked around quick until she saw me, and come and put her hand on my shoulder light and quick and easy as maw herself might 'a' done it.

"Come on," she said. "Let's go home to dinner."

"Nome," I said. "I got to ketch the bus to Jefferson."

"I know. There's plenty of time. We'll go home and eat dinner first."

She had a car. And now we was right down in the middle of all them other cars. We was almost under the busses, and all them crowds of people on the street close enough to where I could have talked to them if I had knowed who they was. After a while she stopped the car. "Here we are," she said, and I looked at it, and if all that was her house, she sho had a big family. But all of it wasn't. We crossed a hall with trees growing in it and went into a little room without nothing in it but a nigger dressed up in a uniform a heap shinier than them soldiers had, and the nigger shut the door, and then I hollered, "Look out!" and grabbed, but it was all right; that whole little room jest went right on up and stopped and the door opened and we was in another hall, and the lady unlocked door and we went in, and there was another soldier, a old feller, with a britching strop, too, and a silver-colored bird on each shoulder.

"Here we are," the lady said. "This is Colonel McKellogg. Now, what would you like for dinner?"

"I reckon I'll jest have some ham and eggs and coffee," I said. She had done started to pick up the telephone. She stopped, "Coffee?" she said.

"When did you start drinking coffee?"

"I don't know," I said. "I reckon it was before I could remember."

"You're about eight, aren't you?" she said.

"Nome," I said. "I'm eight and ten months. Going on eleven months."

She telephoned then. Then we set there and I told them how Pete had jest left that morning for Pearl Harbor and I had aimed to go with him, but I would have to go back home to take care of maw and look after Pete's ten acres, and she said how they had a little boy about my size, too, in a school in the East. Then a nigger, another one, in a short kind of shirttail coat, rolled a kind of wheelbarrer in. It had my ham and eggs and a glass of milk and a piece of pie, too, and I thought I was hungry But when I taken the first bite I found out I couldn't swallow it, and I got up quick.

"I got to go," I said.

"Wait," she said.

"I got to go," I said.

"Just a minute," she said. "I've already telephoned for the car. It won't be but a minute now. Can't you drink the milk even? Or maybe some of your coffee?"

"Nome," I said. "I ain't hungry. I'll eat when I git home."

Then the telephone rung. She never even answered it.

"There," she said. "There's the car." And we went back down in that 'ere little moving room with the dressed-up nigger. This time it was a big car with a soldier driving it. I got into the front with him. She give the soldier a dollar.

"He might get hungry," she said. "Try to find a decent place for him."

"O. K., Mrs. McKellogg," the soldier said.

Then we was gone again. And now I could see Memphis good, bright in the sunshine, while we was swinging around it. And first thing I knowed, we was back on the same highway the bus run on this morning the patches of stores and them big gins and sawmills, and Memphis running on for miles, it seemed like to me, before it begun to give out. Then we was running again between the fields and woods, running fast now, and except for that soldier, it was like I hadn't never been to Memphis a-tall. We was going fast now.

At this rate, before I knowed it we would be home again, and I thought about me riding up to Frenchman's Bend in this big car with a soldier running it, and all of a sudden I begun to cry. I never knowed I was fixing to, and I couldn't stop it. I set there by that soldier, crying. We was going fast.

"Two Soldiers"

PLOT QUIZ

1. "Me and Pete," the first three words of the story, refers to:

(a) Billy Joe and his brother
(b) The narrator and his cousin
(c) The narrator and brother

2. The narrator of the story is almost ________ years old.

(a) Nine
(b) Ten
(c) Fifteen
(d) Seventeen
(e) Twenty

3. Pete is almost ________ years old.

(a) Nine
(b) Ten
(c) Fifteen
(d) Seventeen
(e) Twenty

4. The story takes place in (two answers):

(a) Memphis
(b) Oxford
(c) Frenchman's Bend
(d) Mississippi
(e) Jefferson

5. The time of the story is during the ________.

(a) Revolutionary War
(b) Civil War
(c) First World War
(d) Second World War

6. Pete goes to the city because he had been drafted.

(a) True
(b) False

7. When Pete left home, he was most concerned about the effect his absence would have on his:

(a) Maw
(b) Pap
(c) Brother
(d) Sister
(d) None of these

8. Pete's mother *is against* his leaving home because she:

(a) Can't think of one good reason
(b) Thinks that her brother did enough in WW I
(c) Knows he will get into trouble
(d) Thinks his brother will want to leave home next

9. Pete's father is *against* his leaving home because:

(a) He had done enough already
(b) He needed Pete's help on the farm
(c) He had gotten into trouble himself
(d) He agreed with Pete's mother's thinking
(e) None of these

10. Pete's brother is both *for and against* his brother's leaving home.

(a) True
(b) False

11. Since Pete felt that he had to leave home, that he's "got to go," his brother assumed that he would have to go with him.

(a) True
(b) False

12. Pete never did give a reason for leaving home.

(a) True
(b) False

13. The author wants us to admire Pete's reason for leaving home.

(a) True
(b) False

14. The author wants us to think that Pete's brother is foolish for wanting to leave home with his brother.

(a) True
(b) False

15. Pete's brother finally gets to the city where Pete had gone by:

(a) Walking
(b) Walking and a bus
(c) Hitchhiking
(d) Bus
(e) Train

16. When the narrator finally gets to Memphis and finds his brother, Pete is:

(a) Curious
(b) Astonished
(c) Disgusted
(d) Angry
(e) Embarrassed

17. Pete immediately reprimands his brother for:

(a) Using profane language
(b) Using his knife
(c) Whining and whimpering
(d) Disobeying him
(e) Not telling his parents he had also left home

18. Peter's brother told him that he had come to Memphis because:

(a) He wanted to say goodbye
(b) His heart hurt
(c) He knew he wanted him to come
(d) He knew he would need wood and water
(e) None of these

19. Pete's brother is astonished when his older brother:

(a) Hits him on the head
(b) Takes away his knife
(c) Kisses him
(d) Shouts angrily at him
(e) Tells him the Army had rejected him

20. When Pete's brother returns home, he:

(a) Tells his parents he's sorry for being so late
(b) Begins crying uncontrollably
(c) Tells his parents he wanted to see Pete
(d) Blames Pete for leaving home
(e) None of these.

Socratic Seminar

1. Why is the story told from the view-point of Pete's nine-year-old brother?
2. Why does Faulkner have his narrator speak in dialect?
3. Why does Pete never explain why he *has* to go to war?
4. Why doesn't Pete's mother understand why Pete *has* to go to war?
5. Does Faulkner want us to regard Pete's father as unpatriotic because he can see no use in his son joining the US Army?
6. Why does Pete's brother hold back his tears when Pete gets on the bus to Memphis, but cry uncontrollably when the soldier drives him home to Frenchman's Bend?
7. Why does Faulkner contrast the poverty of the Grier family with the wealth of the Colonel and his wife and son?
8. Why does the movie version omit the scene where Mrs. McKellogg takes Pete's brother to her home for dinner?
9. Why would Faulkner reject the Monterey Home Video version of his story by Christopher Lula?
10. Why would Faulkner approve the Aaron Schneider version of his story?

Two Soldiers

DVD (40 MINS) 2006

Plot summary

Setting: Mississippi 1941 (story published in 1942)

1. "The Lone Ranger" rides again (background music). Unlike the original story which opens with Pete and his little brother sneaking off to listen to Killegrew's radio, the 2004 version begins with Pete and his nearly nine-year-old brother, Willie, examining the nest of a green heron. While looking for a shikepoke egg Pete explains how this bird is special because it returns to the same nest every year. Willie makes a strange offhand comment: "It must be as lazy as Pap."
2. Kiligrew's radio: Flash. Flash. Pearl Harbor: "Yesterday, December 7, 1941, a day which will live in infamy . . . FDR.
3. Pete and Willie try to go to sleep. "Go to sleep. Say your prayers." Pete recalls FDR's memorable words.
4. Pete gives Willie a shikepoke egg and his entire egg collection. "Why don't you want it anymore?" his brother asks.
5. "I don't see a bit of use in this. Who will help me with the plowing? I'll get behind." Pete: "You've been behind as long as I can remember."
6. "You whip the biggins and I'll whip the littens."
7. Maw packs Pete's valise. "You ain't rich and nobody will know where you come from but don't you never forget your heart is as rich as any man's, anywhere."

   Faulkner: "Don't never forget who you are. You ain't rich and the rest of the world outside of Frenchman's Bend never heard of you. But your blood is good as any blood anywhere, and don't you never forget it" (page 87).
8. Paw puts Pete on the Greyhound to Memphis. "Here's your grandpap's watch . . . When Pete says goodbye to Willie, he rubs his head and then says, "Don't forget your prayers."
9. Before Pete leaves the next morning, Willie stands transfixed by his open pocket knife stuck in a log.
10. Supper at home. Lone Ranger rides again. Willie leaves home at night and walks 30 miles to Jefferson which is 50 miles from Memphis. The Law picks up the boy because he is an evident runaway.
11. The Law (Sheriff Foote) takes Willie to the bus depot. The clerk also wants to swap Willie's egg but he will do so only for a bus ticket to Memphis. When the clerk tries to stop Willie from leaving the room, he threatens him with his pocket knife.
12. While waiting for the social worker to arrive, does Willie understand the sheriff's joke about a skunk? ("The skunk tunk that the stump stunk but the stump thunk the skunk stunk.")

13. After Mrs. Habersham, the social worker arrives, and is repulsed by the "malodorous" boy, she makes a grand display of charity by buying his ticket.
14. On the bus to Memphis, a black guitar player sings "Hold that tiger."
15. In Memphis, after Willie finds the Army registration, he begins calling out Pete's name along a long line of men waiting to sign up. Frustrated, he bursts into the courthouse shouting, "Where's Pete? Pete Grier? He's goin to war in Pearl Harbor and I'm goin too!"
16. An angry sergeant tells Pete the best way he can help Pete is to "GO HOME!" Another sergeant tries to get rid of Willie by telling him that they have no more pint-size uniforms. Finally, when a major tries to grab Willie, he pulls his knife on him, cutting his hand.
17. Colonel McKellog enters to investigate the ruckus. He tells Willie that we don't attack unarmed men. He hands him his knife. How did you get here? He walked?! How far is Jefferson? How old are you? What do you plan to do in the Army?
18. The Colonel orders the Major to bring Willie's brother to his office. Lone Ranger theme.
19. When Pete enters, the Colonel tells him there's no need for him to apologize for his little brother.
20. Pete asks Willie what he is doing here and then tells the Colonel that he got into his stubborn little head that he was gonna be a soldier. When Pete again asks Willie why he's here, he replies simply, "It hurt my heart."
21. Moved, when Pete makes Willie promise that he will go home, Willie responds, "You ain't comin back, are you?"
22. The Colonel tells Willie that he can watch the big bird (DC 3) that will take Pete to Little Rock.
23. Pete breaks down and kisses Willie. Don't forget the way home. I'll never forget. It's instinct.
24. As a soldier begins driving Willie back to Frenchman's Bend, Willie jumps out of the moving car and begins walking. The Colonel get out of the car, walks quickly after Willie, and asks where he is going. He replies, "I got to get home, today." When he replies that the Colonel asks if he wants to see his brother leave for Little Rock on the silver bird? When Willie refuses, the Colonel orders the soldier to begin the three-hour drive back to Frenchmen's Bend and then returns his pocket knife.
25. Closing scenes:
    - Pete boards the DC 3 to Little Rock.
    - Willie begins crying uncontrollably on his way back to Frenchmen's Bend.
    - Closing image: Pete hoists Willie on his shoulders and walks down a hill.

Note: For the sequel, "Shall not Perish," published in 1943, Faulkner wrote a TV play for Lux Video Theater in 1954.

Barack Obama's Speech on Patriotism

Independence, MO:

June 30, 2008

Precis

Introduction (1–4)

"A shot heard around the world."

In 1775, a band of Lexington and Concord colonists fired "a shot heard around the world" that began the American Revolution and America's experiment in democracy. The odds against them were enormous, for ultimate failure would bring charges of treason and death by hanging. And yet they took that chance. They did so not on behalf of a particular tribe or lineage, but on behalf of a larger idea: the idea of liberty, the idea of God-given, inalienable rights.

Those men of Lexington and Concord were among our first patriots. And at the beginning of a week when we celebrate the birth of our nation, I think it's fitting to pause for a moment and reflect on the meaning of patriotism, theirs and ours—about the commitments that bind us together as a nation and that bind us to each other as well.

The meaning of patriotism today (5–7)

How do we keep ourselves safe and secure while preserving our liberties? How do we restore trust in a government that seems increasingly removed from its people and dominated by special interests? How do we ensure that, in an increasingly global economy, the winners maintain allegiance to the less fortunate? How do we resolve our differences at a time of increasing diversity? And finally it's worth considering the meaning of patriotism on this anniversary of the birth of our nation and while we are in the midst of a crucial presidential election, because the question of who is or is not a patriot all too often poisons our political debates in ways that divide us rather than bring us together.

My patriotism now questioned (8–10)

Throughout my life, I've always taken my deep and abiding love for this country as a given. It was how I was raised; it is what propelled me into public service; it is why I am running for president. And yet, during the last sixteen months, for the first time my patriotism has been challenged. So let me say this at the outset of my remarks: I will never question the patriotism of others in this campaign. And I will not stand idly by when I hear others question mine.

Patriotism then and now (11–14)

My concerns here aren't simply personal, however. After all, throughout our history, men and women of far greater significance and stature than me have had their patriotism questioned in the midst of momentous debates.

Thomas Jefferson was accused by the Federalists of selling out to the French; the Anti-Federalists were just as convinced that John Adams was in cahoots with the British, intent on restoring monarchal rule. Likewise, even our wisest presidents have sought sometimes to justify questionable practices on the basis of patriotism: Adams' Alien and Sedition Act, Lincoln's suspension of habeas corpus, Roosevelt's internment of Japanese-Americans during World War II.

All were defended at the time as expressions of patriotism, and those who disagreed with their policies were sometimes labeled as unpatriotic. In other words, the use of patriotism as a political sword or a political shield is as old as the republic.

Still, what's striking about today's patriotism debate is the degree to which it remains rooted in the culture wars of the 1960s, in the arguments that go back 40 years or more.

In the early years of the civil rights movement and the opposition to the Vietnam War, defenders of the status quo often accused anybody who questioned the wisdom of government policies of being unpatriotic. Meanwhile, some of those in the so-called counterculture of the '60s reacted not merely by criticizing particular government policies, but by attacking the symbols, and in extreme cases the very idea of America itself.

Patriotism remains a divisive issue (15–18)

Most Americans never bought into these simplistic world views, these caricatures of left and of right. Most Americans understood that dissent does not make one unpatriotic . . . and most Americans understand that there's nothing smart or sophisticated about a cynical disregard for America's traditions and institutions.

Given the enormous challenges that lie before us, we can no longer afford these sorts of divisions. None of us expect that arguments about patriotism will, or should, vanish entirely. After all, when we argue about patriotism, we're arguing about who we are as a country and, more importantly, who we should be. But surely we can agree that no party or political philosophy has a monopoly on patriotism. And surely we can arrive at a definition of patriotism that, however rough and imperfect, captures the best of America's common spirit.

What is patriotism? (19–20)

What would such a definition look like? For me, as for most Americans, patriotism starts as a gut instinct, a loyalty and love for country that's rooted in some of my earliest memories.

The story of my patriotism (21–24)

I remember listening to my grandmother telling stories about her work on a bomber assembly line during World War II. I remember my grandfather handing me his dog tags from his time in Patton's army and understanding that his defense of this country marked one of his greatest sources of pride. That's my idea of America.

I remember, when living for four years in Indonesia as a child, I listened to my mother reading me the first lines of the Declaration of Independence, "We hold these truths to be self-evident, that all men are created equal, that they're endowed by their creator with certain unalienable rights, that among these are life, liberty and the pursuit of happiness."

I remember her explaining how this declaration applied to every American and how those words and the words of the United States Constitution protected us from the injustices that we witnessed other people suffering during those years abroad.

What my patriotism means to me today (25–29)

As I got older, that gut instinct that so many of us have, that America is the greatest country on Earth, would survive. That instinct that this is the greatest country on Earth survived not only because, in my mind, the joys of American life and culture—its vitality, its variety, its freedom—always outweighed its imperfections, but because I learned that what makes America great has never been its perfection, but the belief that it can be made better.

You know, for a young man like me of mixed race, without firm anchor in any particular community, without even a father's steadying hand, it is this essential American idea—that we are not constrained by the accident of birth, but can make of our lives what we will—that has defined my life, just as it has defined the life of so many other Americans.

And that's why, for me, patriotism is always more than just loyalty to a place on a map or a certain kind of people. Instead, it's also loyalty to

America's ideals, ideals for which anyone can sacrifice, or defend, or give their last full measure of devotion.

America's imperfections call for the patriotism of dissent (30–35)

I believe it is this loyalty that allows a country teeming with different races and ethnicities, religions and customs, to come together as one. I believe also that those who attack America's flaws without acknowledging the singular greatness of our ideals, and their proven capacity to inspire a better world, do not truly understand America.

Of course, precisely because America isn't perfect, precisely because our ideals constantly demand more from us, patriotism can never be defined as loyalty to any particular leader, or government, or policy.

Now, we may hope that our leaders and our government stand up for our ideals, stand up for what's right, and there are many times in our history when that's occurred. But when our laws, when our leaders or our government are out of alignment with those ideals, then the dissent of ordinary Americans may prove to be one of the truest expressions of patriotism.

Patriotism also means personal sacrifice and service (36–43)

Beyond a loyalty to America's ideals, beyond a willingness to dissent on behalf of those ideals, I also believe that patriotism must, if it is to mean anything, involve the willingness to sacrifice, to give up something we value on behalf of a larger cause.

Indeed, one of the good things to emerge from the current conflict in Iraq has been the widespread recognition that, whether you support this war or oppose it, the sacrifice of our troops is always worthy of honor. That's a change from the '60s that's been very welcome to many of us.

But for the rest of us, for those of us not in uniform or without loved ones in the military, the call to service for the country's greater good remains an imperative of citizenship. Sadly, in recent years, in the midst of war on two fronts, this call to service never came.

I believe one of the tasks of the next administration is to ensure that this movement towards service grows and sustains itself in the years to come.

We should expand AmeriCorps and grow the Peace Corps. We should encourage national service by making it a part of the requirement for a new college assistance program, even as we strengthen the benefits for those whose sense of duty has already led them to serve in our military.

So government can do its part. We must remember, though, that true patriotism cannot be forced or legislated with a mere set of government programs. Instead, it must reside in the hearts of our people, and cultivated in the heart of our culture, and nurtured in the hearts of our children.

Genuine patriotism is the result of good civic education (44–49)

As we begin our fourth century as a nation, it is easy to take the extraordinary nature of America for granted. But it is our responsibility as Americans and as parents to instill that history in our children, both at home and at school.

The loss of quality civic education from so many of our classrooms has left too many young Americans without the most basic knowledge of who our forefathers are, or what they did, or the significance of the founding documents that bear their names. Too many children are ignorant of the sheer effort, the risks and sacrifices made by previous generations, to ensure that this country survived war and depression, through the great struggles of civil, and social, and workers' rights. It is up to us, then, to teach them.

It is up to us to teach our children a lesson that those of us in politics all too often forget: that patriotism involves not only defending this country against external threat, but also working constantly to make America a better place for future generations.

When we fail to educate effectively millions of our children so that they might compete in a global economy or we fail to invest in the basic scientific research that has driven innovation in this country, we risk leaving behind an America that has fallen in the ranks of the world.

Genuine patriotism also has an eye on posterity (50–53)

Just as patriotism involves each of us making a commitment to this nation that extends beyond our own individual immediate self-interest, so must that commitment extend beyond our own time here on Earth. Our greatest leaders have always understood this. They've defined patriotism with an eye towards posterity.

George Washington is rightly revered for his leadership of the Continental Army, but one of his greatest acts of patriotism was his insistence on stepping down after two terms, reminding future presidents that this is a government of and by and for the people.

Abraham Lincoln did not simply win a war or hold the union together. In his unwillingness to demonize those against whom he fought, in his refusal to succumb to either the hatred or self-righteousness that war can unleash, in his ultimate insistence that in the aftermath of war the nation would no longer remain half-slave and half-free, in his trust in the better angels of our nature, Lincoln displayed the wisdom and courage that sets a standard for patriotism.

And it was the most famous son of Independence, Harry S. Truman, who sat in the White House during his final days in office and said in his farewell address, "When Franklin Roosevelt died, I felt there must be a million men better qualified than I to take up the presidential task. But through all of it, through all the years I have worked here in this room, I have been well aware than I did not really work alone, that you were working with me. No president could ever hope to lead our country or to sustain the burdens of this office, save the people helped with their support."

Patriotism is faith in the American people (54–57)

In the end . . . That's what Truman said. And in the end, it may be this quality that best describes patriotism in my mind, not just a love of America in the abstract, but a very particular love for, and faith in, the American people. For we know that the greatness of this country, all result from the energy and imagination of the American people, their toil, drive, struggle, their restlessness and humor and quiet heroism.

That's the liberty we defend, the liberty of each of us to pursue our own dreams. That's the equality we seek, not an equality of results, but the chance of every single one of us to make it if we try.

That's the community we strive to build, one in which we trust in this sometimes messy democracy of ours, one in which we continue to insist that there is nothing we cannot do when we put our mind to it, one in which we see ourselves as part of a larger story, our own fates wrapped up in the fates of those who share allegiance to America's happy and singular creed.

That's what patriotism means to me. Thank you, Independence. God bless you, and may God bless the United States of America.

Bumper Sticker
Patriotism vs. Memorable Rhetoric

JOURNAL WRITING

Questions: To what historic events do these slogans or quotations refer? To whom have some of the slogans or quotations been attributed? Which of these tone words reveal the author's tone or attitude in each statement or slogan?

insidious	laudatory	simplistic	inspiring
elegiac	false analogy	divisive	bigoted
chauvinistic	either/or fallacy	intolerant	jingoistic

1. "My country, right or wrong."
2. "America—Love it or Leave it!"
3. "I only regret that I have but one life to lose for my country."
4. "No one has a right to desecrate the flag."
5. "Bring 'em on!"
6. "You're with us [America] or against us!"
7. "America's mission today is to spread God's gift of democracy to other nations."
8. "The last full measure of devotion"
9. "We few, we happy few, we band of brothers. For he today that sheds his blood with me shall forever be my brother."
10. "All you have to do [to go to war] is tell the common people that they are being attacked or will be attacked and then denounce the pacifists for lack of patriotism and exposing the country to danger. It works the same in any country."
11. "Never was so much owed by so many to so few."

12. “The only thing we have to fear—is fear itself.”

13. “Ask not what your country can do for you. Ask what you can do for your country”

14. “Patriotism is the last refuge of a scoundrel.”

15. “Patriotism is not the last resort of a scoundrel but the first.”

16. “No soldier *wants* to die for his country. Your job is to make the other SOB die for his!”

17. “Love of patriotism becomes a demon when it becomes a god.”

18. “We should not ask if God is on our side but whether we are on His side.”

19. “God Bless America” vs. “God Save America”

20. “Support our troops.”

Socratic Seminar

"Gaston"

Basic Question 1: Does Saroyan want us to conclude that the daughter or the father has more in common with Gaston's situation?

If the daughter has more in common with Gaston, then:

1. Why does the father describe Gaston as "the grand *boulevardier*"?
2. Does he fail to explain what a grand boulevardier is because he thinks the term applies only to himself?
3. Unlike the girl who wants to squash Gaston because he is ugly, why does the father think he is handsome?
4. Is the father trying to tell his daughter that she, like Gaston, is "out in the world and on [her] own now"?
5. Why does the father say that Gaston could only TRY to live in their house?
6. Why does the father think it unfair for people to holler when someone comes out of his house?
7. Why does the girl describe Gaston's house as "broken"?

If the father has more in common with Gaston, then:

8. Why does the girl ask **who** the bug is rather than **what** it is?
9. Why does the author imply that the girl is as confused as Gaston?
10. Why does the girl begin to adopt her father's view of Gaston?
11. Why does the girl cry just before she kills Gaston?
12. Why does the girl say that her father's house is like Gaston's?
13. Near the end of the story, why does Saroyan refer to the father as "the man"?
14. Why does the story end with the father feeling only "a little" like the squash Gaston?

Basic Question 2: Why does the father let his daughter make up her own mind instead of telling her what to do?

Basic Question 3: Does the author intend the little girl's situation to be like Gaston's?

Basic Question 4: Why would the father but not the mother of their six-year-old daughter understand Khalil Gibran's poem?

"Gaston" may well be William Saroyan's best-known and loved story that contrasts the parents of their six-year-old daughter who visits her "Stranger" father in Paris with her manipulative mother who lives in New York.

After discussion of basic question 1 (Does Saroyan want us to conclude that the daughter or father has more in common with Gaston's situation?), an apt follow up is this poem:

On Children

Khalil Gibran

Your children are not your children.
They are the sons and daughters of Life's longing for itself.
They come through you but not from you,
And though they are with you yet they do not belong to you.
You may give them your love but not your thoughts,
For they have their own thoughts.
You may house their bodies but not their souls,
For their souls dwell in the house of tomorrow,
which you cannot visit, not even in your dreams.
You may strive to be like them,
but seek not to make them like you.
For life goes not backward nor tarries with yesterday.

Note: Khalil Gibran is a Christian Lebanese artist, poet, writer, philosopher, and theologian who came to Boston in 1902 and died in New York in 1931. His best-known book, *The Prophet,* is a series of poetic essays on aspects of everyday life. His books have sold nearly ten million copies in the English language alone.

He is the third-best selling poet in history after Shakespeare and Laozi. When our first child was born, a dear friend gave us a framed copy of Gibran's poem "On Children." My wife and I have tried to follow the wisdom of this mystic poet. When I first read "On Children," I thought immediately of Saroyan's "Gaston" and then began to follow it up with a discussion of the father's and the mother's response to it.

CHAPTER

11 Lesson Plan 9

Is Technology as Much a Curse as a Blessing?

Ray Bradbury, "The Veldt"

1. **Focus:**	Journal: Would you like to have a four-wall television that would produce whatever your thoughts wanted to appear? If so, why so? If not, why not?
2. **Objective:**	To resolve a basic question of interpretation about the overall meaning of the story.
3. **Purpose:**	To increase our mutual understanding (comprehension) and, as a result, our enjoyment of the story. To develop the habit of independent and critical thinking.
4. **Input:**	Plot-check Quiz on Three Kinds of Questions and Exercise on the Qualities of Good Discussion Questions on the story by Bradbury.
5. **Modeling, checking, and guided practice:**	During discussion the co-leaders *model* the Four Rules of Socratic Discussion by asking follow-up questions for clarification, substantiation, consistency, relevance, implication, resolution, and to get more opinion. *Guided practice* **is** the discussion.
6. **Closure:**	Oral or written resolution of one or two basic questions just discussed.
Text:	Ray Bradbury (1965). "The Veldt," *The Vintage Bradbury*. New York: Random House.
Film:	The Ray Bradbury Theatre: "The Veldt" (30 mins) November 1989.
Characters:	George Hadley—although the father of Peter and Wendy marvels at the mechanical genius who had conceived their Happy Life Home, he is

worried that their children have become obsessed with one room, the nursery.

Lydia Hadley—George's wife is more concerned than he about their children's mental health. Indeed, she believes that the nursery has become a surrogate parent.

Peter Hadley—The ten-year-old son who tells his father that he hates him when he realizes that he plans to shut down the nursery.

Wendy Hadley—The twin sister of Peter who is also a obsessed with the nursery.

Mr. McClean—George turns to David McClean, a psychologist, for analysis of the nursery and advice about how he can help his children who are as out of control as the nursery seems to be.

The Veldt

Ray Bradbury

"George, I wish you'd look at the nursery."

"What's wrong with it?"

"I don't know."

"Well, then."

"I just want you to look at it, is all, or call a psychologist in to look at it."

"What would a psychologist want with a nursery?"

"You know very well what he'd want." His wife paused in the middle of the kitchen and watched the stove busy humming to itself, making supper for four.

"It's just that the nursery is different now than it was."

"All right, let's have a look."

They walked down the hall of their soundproofed Happy Life Home, which had cost them thirty thousand dollars installed, this house which clothed and fed and rocked them to sleep and played and sang and was good to them. Their approach sensitized a switch somewhere and the nursery light flicked on when they came within ten feet of it. Similarly, behind them, in the halls, lights went on and off as they left them behind, with a soft automaticity.

"Well," said George Hadley.

They stood on the thatched floor of the nursery. It was forty feet across by forty feet long and thirty feet high; it had cost half again as much as the rest of the house. "But nothing's too good for our children," George had said.

The nursery was silent. It was empty as a jungle glade at hot high noon. The walls were blank and two dimensional. Now, as George and Lydia Hadley stood in the center of the room, the walls began to purr and recede into crystalline distance, it seemed, and presently an African veldt appeared, in three dimensions, on all sides, in color reproduced to the final pebble and bit of straw. The ceiling above them became a deep sky with a hot yellow sun. George Hadley felt the perspiration start on his brow.

"Let's get out of this sun," he said. "This is a little too real. But I don't see anything wrong."

"Wait a moment, you'll see," said his wife. Now the hidden odorphonics were beginning to blow a wind of odor at the two people in the middle of the baked veldtland. The hot straw smell of lion grass, the cool green smell of the hidden water hole, the great rusty smell of animals, the smell of dust like a red paprika in the hot air. And now the sounds: the thump of distant antelope feet on grassy sod, the papery rustling of vultures. A shadow passed through the sky. The shadow flickered on George Hadley's upturned, sweating face.

"Filthy creatures," he heard his wife say.

"The vultures."

"You see, there are the lions, far over, that way. Now they're on their way to the water hole. They've just been eating," said Lydia. "I don't know what."

"Some animal." George Hadley put his hand up to shield off the burning light from his squinted eyes. "A zebra or a baby giraffe, maybe."

"Are you sure?" His wife sounded peculiarly tense.

"No, it's a little late to be sure," he said, amused. "Nothing over there I can see but cleaned bone, and the vultures dropping for what's left."

"Did you hear that scream?" she asked.

"No."

"About a minute ago?"

"Sorry, no."

The lions were coming. And again George Hadley was filled with admiration for the mechanical genius who had conceived this room. A miracle of efficiency selling for an absurdly low price. Every home should have one. Oh, occasionally they frightened you with their clinical accuracy, they startled you, gave you a twinge, but most of the time what fun for everyone, not only your own son and daughter, but for yourself when you felt like a quick jaunt to a foreign land, a quick change of scenery. Well, here it was!

And here were the lions now, fifteen feet away, so real, so feverishly and startlingly real that you could feel the prickling fur on your hand, and your mouth was stuffed with the dusty upholstery smell of their heated pelts, and the yellow of them was in your eyes like the yellow of an exquisite French tapestry, the yellows of lions and summer grass, and the sound of the matted lion lungs exhaling on the silent noontide, and the smell of meat from the panting, dripping mouths. The lions stood looking at George and Lydia Hadley with terrible green-yellow eyes.

"Watch out!" screamed Lydia.

The lions came running at them.

Lydia bolted and ran. Instinctively, George sprang after her. Outside, in the hall, with the door slammed he was laughing and she was crying, and they both stood appalled at the other's reaction.

"George!"

"Lydia! Oh, my dear poor sweet Lydia!"

"They almost got us!"

"Walls, Lydia, remember; crystal walls, that's all they are. Oh, they look real, I must admit—Africa in your parlor—but it's all dimensional, super reactionary, supersensitive color film and metal tape film behind glass screens. It's all odorphonics and sonics, Lydia. Here's my handkerchief."

"I'm afraid." She came to him and put her body against him and cried steadily. "Did you see? Did you feel? It's too real."

"Now, Lydia ..."

"You've got to tell Wendy and Peter not to read any more on Africa."

"Of course—of course." He patted her.

"Promise?"

"Sure."

"And lock the nursery for a few days until I get my nerves settled."

"You know how difficult Peter is about that. When I punished him a month ago by locking the nursery for even a few hours—the tantrum he threw! And Wendy too. They live for the nursery."

"It's got to be locked, that's all there is to it."

"All right" Reluctantly he locked the huge door. "You've been working too hard. You need a rest."

"I don't know—I don't know," she said, blowing her nose, sitting down in a chair that immediately began to rock and comfort her. "Maybe I don't have enough to do. Maybe I have time to think too much. Why don't we shut the whole house off for a few days and take a vacation?"

"You mean you want to fry my eggs for me?"

"Yes." She nodded.

"And darn my socks?"

"Yes." A frantic, watery-eyed nodding.

"And sweep the house?"

"Yes, yes—oh, yes!"

"But I thought that's why we bought this house, so we wouldn't have to do anything?"

"That's just it. I feel like I don't belong here. The house is wife and mother now, and nursemaid. Can I compete with an African veldt? Can I give a bath and scrub the children as efficiently or quickly as the automatic scrub bath can? I cannot. And it isn't just me. It's you. You've been awfully nervous lately."

"I suppose I have been smoking too much."

"You look as if you didn't know what to do with yourself in this house, either. You smoke a little more every morning and drink a little more every afternoon and need a little more sedative every night. You're beginning to feel unnecessary too."

"Am I?" He paused and tried to feel into himself to see what was really there.

"Oh, George!" She looked beyond him, at the nursery door. "Those lions can't get out of there, can they?"

He looked at the door and saw it tremble as if something had jumped against it from the other side.

"Of course not," he said.

At dinner they ate alone, for Wendy and Peter were at a special plastic carnival across town and had televised home to say they'd be late, to go ahead eating. So George Hadley, bemused, sat watching the dining-room table produce warm dishes of food from its mechanical interior.

"We forgot the ketchup," he said.

"Sorry," said a small voice within the table, and ketchup appeared.

As for the nursery, thought George Hadley, it won't hurt for the children to be locked out of it awhile. Too much of anything isn't good for anyone. And it was clearly indicated that the children had been spending a little too much time on Africa. That sun. He could feel it on his neck, still, like a hot paw. And the lions. And the smell of blood. Remarkable how the nursery caught the telepathic emanations of the children's minds and created life to fill their every desire. The children thought lions, and there were lions. The children thought zebras, and there were zebras. Sun—sun. Giraffes—giraffes. Death and death.

That last. He chewed tastelessly on the meat that the table had cut for him. Death thoughts. They were awfully young, Wendy and Peter, for death thoughts. Or, no, you were never too young, really. Long before you knew what death was you were wishing it on someone else. When you were two years old you were shooting people with cap pistols.

But this—the long, hot African veldt—the awful death in the jaws of a lion. And repeated again and again.

"Where are you going?"

He didn't answer Lydia. Preoccupied, he let the lights glow softly on ahead of him, extinguish behind him as he padded to the nursery door. He listened against it. Far away, a lion roared. He unlocked the door and opened it. Just before he stepped inside, he heard a faraway scream. And then another roar from the lions, which subsided quickly. He stepped into Africa. How many times in the last year had he opened this door and found Wonderland, Alice, the Mock Turtle, or Aladdin and his Magical Lamp, or Jack Pumpkin head of Oz, or Dr. Doolittle, or the cow jumping over a very real-appearing moon—all the delightful contraptions of a make-believe world. How often had he seen Pegasus flying in the sky ceiling, or seen fountains of red fire-works, or heard angel voices singing. But now, is yellow hot Africa, this bake oven with murder in the heat. Perhaps Lydia was right. Perhaps they needed a little vacation from the fantasy which was growing a bit too real for ten-year-old children. It was all right to exercise one's mind with gymnastic fantasies, but when the lively child mind settled on one pattern . . .? It seemed that, at a distance, for the past month, he had heard lions roaring, and smelled their strong odor seeping as far away as his study door. But, being busy, he had paid it no attention.

George Hadley stood on the African grassland alone. The lions looked up from their feeding, watching him. The only flaw to the illusion was the open door through which he could see his wife, far down the dark hall, like a framed picture, eating her dinner abstractedly.

"Go away," he said to the lions.

They did not go.

He knew the principle of the room exactly. You sent out your thoughts. Whatever you thought would appear. "Let's have Aladdin and his lamp," he snapped. The veldtland remained; the lions remained.

"Come on, room! I demand Aladdin!" he said.

Nothing happened. The lions mumbled in their baked pelts.

"Aladdin!"

He went back to dinner. "The fool room's out of order," he said. "It won't respond."

"Or—"

"Or what?"

"Or it can't respond," said Lydia, "because the children have thought about Africa and lions and killing so many days that the room's in a rut."

"Could be."

"Or Peter's set it to remain that way."

"Set it?"

"He may have got into the machinery and fixed something."

"Peter doesn't know machinery."

"He's a wise one for ten. That I.Q. of his—"

"Nevertheless—"

"Hello, Mom. Hello, Dad."

The Hadleys turned. Wendy and Peter were coming in the front door, cheeks like peppermint candy, eyes like bright blue agate marbles, a smell of ozone on their jumpers from their trip in the helicopter.

"You're just in time for supper," said both parents.

"We're full of strawberry ice cream and hot dogs," said the children, holding hands. "But we'll sit and watch."

"Yes, come tell us about the nursery," said George Hadley.

The brother and sister blinked at him and then at each other.

"Nursery?"

"All about Africa and everything," said the father with false joviality.

"I don't understand," said Peter.

"Your mother and I were just traveling through Africa with rod and reel; Tom Swift and his Electric Lion," said George Hadley.

"There's no Africa in the nursery," said Peter simply.

"Oh, come now, Peter. We know better."

"I don't remember any Africa," said Peter to Wendy. "Do you?"

"No."

"Run see and come tell."

She obeyed.

"Wendy, come back here!" said George Hadley, but she was gone. The house lights followed her like a flock of fireflies. Too late, he realized he had forgotten to lock the nursery door after his last inspection.

"Wendy'll look and come tell us," said Peter.

"She doesn't have to tell me. I've seen it."

"I'm sure you're mistaken, Father."

"I'm not, Peter. Come along now."

But Wendy was back. "It's not Africa," she said breathlessly.

"We'll see about this," said George Hadley, and they all walked down the hall together and opened the nursery door.

There was a green, lovely forest, a lovely river, a purple mountain, high voices singing, and Rima, lovely and mysterious, lurking in the trees with colorful flights of butterflies, like animated bouquets, lingering in her long hair. The African veldtland was gone. The lions were gone. Only Rima was here now, singing a song so beautiful that it brought tears to your eyes. George Hadley looked in at the changed scene.

"Go to bed," he said to the children.

They opened their mouths.

"You heard me," he said.

They went off to the air closet, where a wind sucked them like brown leaves up the flue to their slumber rooms.

George Hadley walked through the singing glade and picked up something that lay in the comer near where the lions had been. He walked slowly back to his wife.

"What is that?" she asked.

"An old wallet of mine," he said.

He showed it to her. The smell of hot grass was on it and the smell of a lion. There were drops of saliva on it, it bad been chewed, and there were blood smears on both sides. He closed the nursery door and locked it, tight. In the middle of the night he was still awake and he knew his wife was awake. "Do you think Wendy changed it?" she said at last, in the darkroom.

"Of course."

"Made it from a veldt into a forest and put Rima there instead of lions?"

"Yes."

"Why?"

"I don't know. But it's staying locked until I find out."

"How did your wallet get there?"

"I don't know anything," he said, "except that I'm beginning to be sorry we bought that room for the children. If children are neurotic at all, a room like that—"

"It's supposed to help them work off their neuroses in a healthful way."

"I'm starting to wonder." He stared at the ceiling.

"We've given the children everything they ever wanted. Is this our reward—secrecy, disobedience?"

"Who was it said, 'Children are carpets, they should be stepped on occasionally'? We've never lifted a hand. They're insufferable—let's admit it. They come and go when they like; they treat us as if we were offspring. They're spoiled and we're spoiled."

"They've been acting funny ever since you forbade them to take the rocket to New York a few months ago."

"They're not old enough to do that alone, I explained."

"Nevertheless, I've noticed they've been decidedly cool toward us since."

"I think I'll have David McClean come tomorrow morning to have a look at Africa."

"But it's not Africa now, it's Green Mansions country and Rima."

"I have a feeling it'll be Africa again before then."

A moment later they heard the screams.

Two screams. Two people screaming from downstairs. And then a roar of lions.

"Wendy and Peter aren't in their rooms," said his wife.

He lay in his bed with his beating heart. "No," he said. "They've broken into the nursery."

"Those screams—they sound familiar."

"Do they?"

"Yes, awfully."

And although their beds tried very hard, the two adults couldn't be rocked to sleep for another hour. A smell of cats was in the night air.

"Father?" said Peter.

"Yes."

Peter looked at his shoes. He never looked at his father any more, nor at his mother. "You aren't going to lock up the nursery for good, are you?"

"That all depends."

"On what?" snapped Peter.

"On you and your sister. If you intersperse this Africa with a little variety—oh, Sweden perhaps, or Denmark or China—"

"I thought we were free to play as we wished."

"You are, within reasonable bounds."

"What's wrong with Africa, Father?"

"Oh, so now you admit you have been conjuring up Africa, do you?"

"I wouldn't want the nursery locked up," said Peter coldly. "Ever."

"Matter of fact, we're thinking of turning the whole house off for about a month. Live sort of a carefree one-for-all existence."

"That sounds dreadful! Would I have to tie my own shoes instead of letting the shoe tier do it? And brush my own teeth and comb my hair and give myself a bath?"

"It would be fun for a change, don't you think?"

"No, it would be horrid. I didn't like it when you took out the picture painter last month."

"That's because I wanted you to learn to paint all by yourself, son."

"I don't want to do anything but look and listen and smell; what else is there to do?"

"All right, go play in Africa."

"Will you shut off the house sometime soon?"

"We're considering it."

"I don't think you'd better consider it any more, Father."

"I won't have any threats from my son!"

"Very well." And Peter strolled off to the nursery.

"Am I on time?" said David McClean.

"Breakfast?" asked George Hadley.

"Thanks, had some. What's the trouble?"

"David, you're a psychologist."

"I should hope so."

"Well, then, have a look at our nursery. You saw it a year ago when you dropped by; did you notice anything peculiar about it then?"

"Can't say I did; the usual violences, a tendency toward a slight paranoia here or there, usual in children because they feel persecuted by parents constantly, but, oh, really nothing."

They walked down the hall. "I locked the nursery up," explained the father, "and the children broke back into it during the night. I let them stay so they could form the patterns for you to see."

There was a terrible screaming from the nursery.

"There it is," said George Hadley. "See what you make of it."

They walked in on the children without rapping.

The screams had faded. The lions were feeding.

"Run outside a moment, children," said George Hadley. "No, don't change the mental combination. Leave the walls as they are. Get!"

With the children gone, the two men stood studying the lions clustered at a distance, eating with great relish whatever it was they had caught.

"I wish I knew what it was," said George Hadley. "Sometimes I can almost see. Do you think if I brought high-powered binoculars here and—"

David McClean laughed dryly. "Hardly." He turned to study all four walls. "How long has this been going on?"

"A little over a month."

"It certainly doesn't feel good."

"I want facts, not feelings."

"My dear George, a psychologist never saw a fact in his life. He only hears about feelings; vague things. This doesn't feel good, I tell you. Trust my hunches and my instincts. I have a nose for something bad. This is very bad. My advice to you is to have the whole damn room torn down and your children brought to me every day during the next year for treatment."

"Is it that bad?"

"I'm afraid so. One of the original uses of these nurseries was so that we could study the patterns left on the walls by the child's mind, study at our leisure, and help the child. In this case, however, the room has become a channel toward destructive thoughts, instead of a release away from them."

"Didn't you sense this before?"

"I sensed only that you had spoiled your children more than most. And now you're letting them down in some way. What way?"

"I wouldn't let them go to New York."

"What else?"

"I've taken a few machines from the house and threatened them, a month ago, with closing up the nursery unless they did their homework. I did close it for a few days to show I meant business."

"Ah, ha!"

"Does that mean anything?"

"Everything. Where before they had a Santa Claus now they have a Scrooge. Children prefer Santas. You've let this room and this house replace you and your wife in your children's affections. This room is their mother and father, far more important in their lives than their real parents. And now you come along and want to shut it off. No wonder there's hatred here.

You can feel it coming out of the sky. Feel that sun. George, you'll have to change your life. Like too many others, you've built it around creature comforts. Why, you'd starve tomorrow if something went wrong in your kitchen. You wouldn't know how to tap an egg. Nevertheless, turn everything off. Start new. It'll take time. But we'll make good children out of bad in a year, wait and see."

"But won't the shock be too much for the children, shutting the room up abruptly, for good?"

"I don't want them going any deeper into this, that's all."

The lions were finished with their red feast.

The lions were standing on the edge of the clearing watching the two men.

"Now I'm feeling persecuted," said McClean. "Let's get out of here. I never have cared for these damned rooms. Make me nervous."

"The lions look real, don't they?" said George Hadley. "I don't suppose there's any way—"

"What?"

"—that they could become real?"

"Not that I know."

"Some flaw in the machinery, a tampering or something?"

"No."

They went to the door.

"I don't imagine the room will like being turned off," said the father.

"Nothing ever likes to die—even a room."

"I wonder if it hates me for wanting to switch it off?"

"Paranoia is thick around here today," said David McClean. "You can follow it like a spoor. Hello." He bent and picked up a bloody scarf. "This yours?"

"No." George Hadley's face was rigid. "It belongs to Lydia."

They went to the fuse box together and threw the switch that killed the nursery. The two children were in hysterics. They screamed and pranced and threw things. They yelled and sobbed and swore and jumped at the furniture.

"You can't do that to the nursery, you can't!"

"Now, children."

The children flung themselves onto a couch, weeping.

"George," said Lydia Hadley, "turn on the nursery, just for a few moments. You can't be so abrupt."

"No."

"You can't be so cruel …"

"Lydia, it's off, and it stays off. And the whole damn house dies as of here and now. The more I see of the mess we've put ourselves in, the more it sickens me. We've been contemplating our mechanical, electronic navels for too long. My God, how we need a breath of honest air!"

And he marched about the house turning off the voice clocks, the stoves, the heaters, the shoe shiners, the shoe lacers, the body scrubbers and swabbers and massagers, and every other machine he could put his hand to. The house was full of dead bodies, it seemed. It felt like a mechanical cemetery. So silent. None of the humming hidden energy of machines waiting to function at the tap of a button.

"Don't let them do it!" wailed Peter at the ceiling, as if he was talking to the house, the nursery. "Don't let Father kill everything." He turned to his father. "Oh, I hate you!"

"Insults won't get you anywhere."

"I wish you were dead!"

"We were, for a long while. Now we're going to really start living. Instead of being handled and massaged, we're going to live."

Wendy was still crying and Peter joined her again. "Just a moment, just one moment, just another moment of nursery," they wailed.

"Oh, George," said the wife, "it can't hurt."

"All right—all right, if they'll just shut up. One minute, mind you, and then off forever."

"Daddy, Daddy, Daddy!" sang the children, smiling with wet faces.

"And then we're going on a vacation. David McClean is coming back in half an hour to help us move out and get to the airport. I'm going to dress. You turn the nursery on for a minute, Lydia, just a minute, mind you."

And the three of them went babbling off while he let himself be vacuumed upstairs through the air flue and set about dressing himself. A minute later Lydia appeared.

"I'll be glad when we get away," she sighed.

"Did you leave them in the nursery?"

"I wanted to dress too. Oh, that horrid Africa. What can they see in it?"

"Well, in five minutes we'll be on our way to Iowa. Lord, how did we ever get in this house? What prompted us to buy a nightmare?"

"Pride, money, foolishness."

"I think we'd better get downstairs before those kids get engrossed with those damned beasts again."

Just then they heard the children calling, "Daddy, Mommy, come quick quick!" They went downstairs in the air flue and ran down the hall. The children were nowhere in sight. "Wendy? Peter!" They ran into the nursery. The veldtland was empty save for the lions waiting, looking at them.

"Peter, Wendy?"

The door slammed.

"Wendy, Peter!"

George Hadley and his wife whirled and ran back to the door.

"Open the door!" cried George Hadley, trying the knob. "Why, they've locked it from the outside! Peter!" He beat at the door. "Open up!"

He heard Peter's voice outside, against the door.

"Don't let them switch off the nursery and the house," he was saying.

Mr. and Mrs. George Hadley beat at the door. "Now, don't be ridiculous, children. It's time to go. Mr. McClean'll be here in a minute and ..."

And then they heard the sounds. The lions on three sides of them, in the yellow veldt grass, padding through the dry straw, rumbling and roaring in their throats. The lions. Mr. Hadley looked at his wife and they turned and looked back at the beasts edging slowly forward crouching, tails stiff. Mr. and Mrs. Hadley screamed. And suddenly they realized why those other screams had sounded familiar.

"Well, here I am," said David McClean in the nursery doorway, "Oh, hello." He stared at the two children seated in the center of the open glade eating a little picnic lunch. Beyond them was the water hole and the yellow veldtland; above was the hot sun. He began to perspire. "Where are your father and mother?"

The children looked up and smiled. "Oh, they'll be here directly."

"Good, we must get going." At a distance Mr. McClean saw the lions fighting and clawing and then quieting down to feed in silence under the shady trees. He squinted at the lions with his hand tip to his eyes. Now the lions were done feeding. They moved to the water hole to drink. A shadow flickered over Mr. McClean's hot face. Many shadows flickered. The vultures were dropping down the blazing sky.

"A cup of tea?" asked Wendy in the silence.

"The Veldt"

PLOT-CHECK QUIZ

Directions: Fill in the gaps in this passage. The answers in the left-hand column may be used only once, more than once, or not at all.

- George Hadley
- Lydia Hadley
- Wendy Hadley
- Peter Hadley
- Happy Life Home
- David McClean
- nursery
- vacation
- screams
- a cup of tea
- hysterics
- psychologist
- mechanical genius
- African veldt
- out of control
- out of film
- scarf
- nothing happened
- sock
- Rima
- Green Mansions
- wallet
- Aladdin
- shoe
- trip to New York
- robot
- television
- rainbow

It (1) __________________ "had cost half as much again as the (2) __________________ but nothing's too good for your children," according to (3) __________________. Unlike (4) __________________, who was filled with admiration for the person (5) __________________ who had conceived the nursery, this person (6) __________________ feared that the nursery was (7) __________________. "They (8) __________________ and (9) __________________ *live f*or the nursery." "I feel like I don't belong here … How can I compete with a (10) __________________?" This statement is made by (11) __________________ to (12) __________________. "He (13) __________________ knew the principle of the room exactly. You sent out your thoughts. Whatever you thought, would appear." When he (14) __________________ demanded that Aladdin and his lamp appear, (15) __________________. The room was (16) __________________. He (17) __________________ was the (18) __________________ who Lydia asked George to have "a look at" the (19) __________________. When George confronted them (20) __________________ and (21) __________________ about the veldt land in the nursery, they told him that there was no veldt land because the room had become (22) __________________. At this point in the story, George found his (23) __________________ in the nursery. On several occasions, George and Lydia heard familiar (24) __________________ coming from the (25) __________________. "I wouldn't want the nursery locked up," said (26) ________________coldly. "Ever." They (27) ________________ and (28) ________________ planned to lock up the nursery for about a month and take a (30) ________________. "I don't want to do anything but look, listen, and smell: what else is there to do?" asked (31) ________________. According to (32) ________________,"the room had become a channel toward destructive thoughts, instead of a release away from them." "I don't imagine (33) ________________ will like being turned off," said (34) ________________. When (35) ________________ and George were examining the room, this time they discovered a bloody (36) ________________ which belonged to (37) ________________. When (38) ________________ "killed" the nursery, they (39) ________________ and (40) ________________ went into a (41) ________________. "Oh, I hate you! I wish you were dead!" said (42) ________________ to (43) ________________. He (44) ________________ momentarily turned the room back on at the request of (45) ________________. When (46) ________________ and (47) ________________ screamed, they suddenly realized why those other screams were now so familiar; they were (48) ________________. The story ends with them (49) ________________ asking (50) ________________ if he would (51) ________________.

Socratic Seminar

Basic Question of Interpretation: Even after the Hadleys realize that the nursery is a real danger, why are they unable to do anything to improve their family life?

1. Why do the Hadleys see the nursery harmful to their children but not to themselves?
2. Why does the nursery fail to respond to George's attempt at change it from a veldt into Aladdin?
3. When the Hadleys believe that their children have broken into the nursery, why do they go back to sleep?
4. Why don't the Hadley's take David McClean's advice to have the nursery torn down and their children brought to him for treatment?
5. Why do the Hadley's continue to give into to their children even after they realize how spoiled they have become?
6. Why does the author have the children kill their parents?
7. Why are Peter and Wendy so calm after killing their parents?
8. Why is the nursery more important to the children than their parents?
9. Why do the children create death scenes in the nursery?
10. Are we to agree with George that the children are too young to know what death is?
11. Why does Bradbury want us to know that before the children had become obsessed with the veldt, they had used the nursery for scenes from famous children's books?
12. Why do the children put their father's wallet and their mother's scarf in the nursery?
13. Why doesn't Bradbury give Mr. McClean a chance to rid the children of their "death thoughts"?
14. Why do George, Lydia, and Peter all refer to the house as if it had a will of its own?
15. Does Bradbury want us to feel sorry for George and Lydia for being unable to help their children have normal lives?
16. Why does the story end with Peter and Wendy asking Mr. McClean to share lunch with them?

Nonfiction Readings

On God, Monsters and Angels; "At play in the fields of the Lord."

RAY BRADBURY (1920–2012)

(CNN) Ray Bradbury lives in a rambling Los Angeles home full of stuffed dinosaurs, a tin robot pushing an ice cream cart, and a life-sized Bullwinkle the Moose doll lounging in a cushioned chair. The 89-year-old science fiction author watches Fox News Channel by day, Turner Classic Movies by night. He spends the rest of his time summoning "the monsters and angels" of his imagination for his enchanting tales.

Bradbury's imagination has yielded classic books such as *Fahrenheit 451, The Martin Chronicles* and 600 short stories that predicted everything from the emergence of ATMs to live broadcasts of fugitive car chases. Bradbury, who turns 90 this month, says he will sometimes open one of his books late at night and cry out thanks to God.

"I sit there and cry because I haven't done any of this," he told Sam Weller, his biographer and friend. "It's a God-given thing, and I'm so grateful, so, so grateful. The best description of my career as a writer is, 'At play in the fields of the Lord.'"

Bradbury's stories are filled with references to God and faith, but he's rarely talked at length about his religious beliefs, until now. He describes himself as a "delicatessen religionist." He's inspired by Eastern and Western religions.

The center of his faith, though, is love. Everything—the reason he decided to write his first short story at 12; his 56-year marriage to his muse and late wife, Maggie; his friendships with everyone from Walt Disney to Alfred Hitchcock—is based on love. Bradbury is in love with love.

Once, when he saw Walt Disney, architect of the Magic Kingdom, Christmas shopping in Los Angeles, Bradbury approached him and said: "Mr. Disney, my name is Ray Bradbury and I love you."

Bradbury's favorite book in the Bible is the Gospel of John, which is filled with references to love. "At the center of religion is love," Bradbury says from his home, which is painted dandelion yellow in honor of his favorite book, *Dandelion Wine.* "I love you and I forgive you. I am like you and you are like me. I love all people. I love the world. I love creating.... Everything in our life should be based on love."

Bradbury's voice booms with enthusiasm over the phone. He now uses a wheelchair. His hearing has deteriorated. But he talks like an excitable kid with an old man's voice. (Each Christmas, Bradbury asked his wife to give him toys in place of any other gifts.)

Weller, author of *Listen to The Echoes: The Ray Bradbury Interviews*, says Bradbury ends many conversations with "God bless." Weller's book devotes an entire chapter to Bradbury's faith. "I once asked him if he prayed, and he said, 'Joy is the grace we say to God,'" Weller says.

Bradbury was raised as a Baptist in Waukegan, Illinois, by his father, a utility lineman, and his mother, a housewife. Both were infrequent churchgoers.

His family moved to Los Angeles during the Great Depression to look for work. When he turned 14, Bradbury began visiting Catholic churches, synagogues, and charismatic churches on his own to figure out his faith. Bradbury has been called a Unitarian, but he rejects that term. He dislikes labels of any kind. "I'm a Zen Buddhist if I would describe myself," he says. "I don't think about what I do. I do it. That's Buddhism. I jump off the cliff and build my wings on the way down."

Bradbury started writing for pulp magazines like *Weird Tales* and *Thrilling Wonder Stories* at the beginning of his career. But even then, faith was an important theme.

In his 1949 story "The Man," Bradbury tells the story of a rocket crew landing on Mars, only to see their thunder taken by a Christ-like figure who had arrived only hours earlier. In subsequent stories such as "Bless Me, Father, For I Have Sinned," priests and other ordinary people search and find redemption.

Allusions to Christianity are common in his stories, but Bradbury doesn't define himself as a Christian. He considers Jesus a wise prophet, like Buddha and Confucius. "Jesus is a remarkable person," Bradbury says. "He was on his way to becoming Christ, and he made it."

Weller, also author of *The Bradbury Chronicles: The Life of Ray Bradbury*, says Bradbury's religious antenna is most attuned to Christianity. "The guy keeps writing about Jesus, but he doesn't consider himself a Christian," Weller says.

"He says faith is necessary but that we should accept the fact that when it comes to God, none of us know anything." The Rev. Calvin Miller, author of the New Testament novels *The Singer Trilogy*, sees an optimism in Bradbury's stories that's reflected in the Judeo-Christian belief that there will be a "new heaven and a new Earth" one day.

Miller once wrote an essay about Bradbury's "Christian positivism," titled "Hope in a Doubtful Age," that was published in *Christianity Today*, an evangelical magazine. After the essay appeared, Miller says, he was sorting through mail at home when he noticed two thank-you letters from Bradbury—one written when the author was headed to Paris for vacation and another when he arrived.

The following Christmas, Miller says, he received something else from Bradbury.

"Every Christmas afterward, he sent me a card," Miller says. "I guess the religious implications of the article meant a lot to him."

The religious implications of space travel also mean much to Bradbury.

Bradbury has been a relentless supporter of space exploration. Ascending to the heavens won't destroy God; it'll reinforce belief, he says. "We're moving more toward God," he says. "We're moving toward more proofs of his creation in other worlds he's created in other parts of the universe. Space travel will increase our belief in God."

As he approaches the end of his journey, Bradbury is still conjuring his monsters and angels. His next book, *Summer Morning, Summer Night,* was just released last month (2010).

Many of his best friends, though, are not around to read him anymore. "My personal telephone book is a book of the dead now," Bradbury told Weller in his book of interviews. "I'm so old. Almost all of my friends have died, and I don't have the guts to take their names out of the book."

Bradbury is also concerned about something beyond his own mortality: humanity's survival. Space travel and religion seek the same goal—immortality, Bradbury says. If humanity remains on Earth, it is doomed because someday the sun will either explode or flame out.

Everyone—not just the characters in his story—must eventually explore the stars, he says. "We must move into the universe. Mankind must save itself. We must escape the danger of war and politics. We must become astronauts and go out into the universe and discover the God in ourselves."

What Will Our Homes Look Like in 2114

Nikki Sheehan

The house builders of the last century had it pretty easy. Essentially, all they had to do was provide pleasant accommodation on budget that wouldn't fall down. But, according to research commissioned by insurers Zurich, and carried out by architectural practice, Arup Associates, the builders of the future will be struggling with issues such as population growth, global warming, and fuel and water crises.

"History shows that we can't predict the future with absolute certainty, but we can prepare for it," says Martin Horsler from Zurich. And it certainly makes sense for insurers to encourage building that will leave them less vulnerable to big payouts for damage caused by changing climatic conditions. So what, according to Zurich, can we expect to see down the average British street in 2107?

Hot Summers, Stormy Winters

The latest projections suggest that by 2080 summers could be up to 7°C warmer, and with temperatures regularly soaring to 35°C and above, simply opening the windows won't cool us down.

To combat this, it's likely that the semi of the future will be built with solar shades to block out 95 per cent of sunlight during the day, and extended overhangs to beat the heat.

Fuel-guzzling air conditioning as we know it will be out, but an eco-friendly alternative will be provided by pipes carrying cool, recycled water built into, and around, ceilings and beams.

While summer and autumn look set to be hot and dry, winters may be wetter with more frequent, intense storms. But the inhabitants of 2107 will hardly notice. According to the Zurich study, the house of the future may be kept warm by gas-filled triple-glazed windows and 'intelligent insulation' that automatically adjusts to external temperatures.

H2O: Water Issues

Despite the lashing rain, long periods of drought are also forecast, and homes may need to be largely independent from the mains.

The homes of tomorrow will be adapted to collect and store rainwater, and will be using sustainable drainage systems, and water recycling.

So you can kiss your power shower goodbye. If water becomes a luxury, dust baths look more likely than bubble baths.

And we can forget our English country gardens. Obviously sprinklers and hose-pipes will be locked in the shed for good, and sun-loving olive trees and cacti could replace the traditional roses and hydrangeas.

But roof gardens are likely to be very common. Living roofs covered in vegetation such as low growing succulents prevent buildings from absorbing too much heat in the summer, and absorb rainfall to lower the risk of flooding in the winter.

Any pitched roofs being built are likely to be inverted for efficient rainwater harvesting. And if, despite our efforts, some areas remain at risk from flooding, houses could be built on stilts.

Microgeneration: Power to the People

Self-sufficiency is the key to our future power needs. On a national level the UK could be growing its own energy thanks to greater use of bio-fuels from plants such as rapeseed.

But the householders of the next century will expect their homes to produce most of the energy their family needs from wind turbines, solar panels and geothermal energy systems

These microgenerating houses may even fuel our cars. No more queuing up at the petrol station: the cars of the future could be battery powered, plugged in and charged at night by our homes.

Modular Homes—Room for the Mother-in-law

Land shortages and an ageing population will intensify the demand for space-saving accommodation that can house several generations of one family. But we're not talking granny flats. Homes of the future could be modular, or even mobile, with walls, rooms and even floors that could be added or taken away to respond to the changing needs of three generations. Here's the good news—put away your tools: the modular hi-tech homes of tomorrow are likely to be too complicated for home maintenance.

Goodbye Commute

The trend has already begun, but in the future it looks likely that advances in technology could create a society of home workers. But this doesn't have to mean social isolation. The experts believe that, as in the past, people spending more time at home will lead to enriched local communities. Shops, services and even our relationship with our neighbours could play a far greater part in our daily lives.

Tomorrow's World Today

Although Zurich's vision may seem futuristic, many people are already investing in tomorrow's technology. Architects are building houses on stilts in high-risk flood areas such as East Anglia, Liverpool and Cornwall. Politicians, among many others, are leading the way in generating their own power by installing microgeneration devices into their own homes. And rainwater-absorbing flat roofs are becoming increasingly common on eco-friendly new builds. As for rushing to redesign our homes so that the mother-in-law can move in, that may still be some way off.

Ten Ways Our Homes Will Change

1. **Modular homes:** Walls, rooms and even floors could be added or taken away to accommodate three generations as we live longer and land becomes more expensive.
2. **Houses on stilts:** In areas particularly at risk of flooding, houses built on stilts could become a common sight.
3. **Death of DIY:** The more hi-tech the house becomes, with solar panels, wind-turbines and geothermal energy systems, the less able we will be at DIY.
4. **Self-heating:** Solar panels, gas-filled triple-glazed windows and intelligent insulation could all be standard fittings and fixtures.
5. **Self-cooling:** Pipes carrying cool, recycled water built into, and around, ceilings and beams; solar shades and houses built with extended overhangs to beat the heat.
6. **Energy self-sufficient:** Renewable energy generated by family wind turbines and solar panels.
7. **Water independent:** Homes tailor-made to reuse and recycle water. In the house of the future, water used and waste produced could be Reese and recycled.
8. **The end of the commute:** Technology could create a commute-free society as more people work from home.
9. **Plug-in cars:** As our homes become power sources in their own right, battery-powered cars will become more common.
10. **Flora and fauna:** Regular droughts and water shortages will mean a shift to more Mediterranean.

CHAPTER

12 Lesson Plan 10

Is the Desire to Excel as Strong as the Tendency to be Mediocre?

"Harrison Bergeron"

1. **Focus:**	Journal: Is the desire to excel as strong in human nature as the tendency to be mediocre?
2. **Objective:**	To resolve a basic question of interpretation about the overall meaning of the story.
3. **Purpose:**	To develop the habits of reflective, critical and independent thinking.
4. **Input:**	Begin with a Plot-check Quiz and then two Review Exercises on: ○ The Three Kinds of Questions ○ Qualities of Good Discussion Questions
5. **Modeling, checking, and guided practice:**	During discussion the co-leaders *model* the Four Rules of Socratic Discussion by asking follow-up questions for clarification, substantiation, consistency, relevance, implication, resolution, and to get more opinion. *Guided practice* **is** the discussion.
6. **Closure:**	Oral or written resolution of one or two basic questions.
Text:	Kurt Vonnegut (1981), "Harrison Bergeron," *Short Stories: Characters in Conflict* (J. Warriner, Ed.). New York: HarcourtBraceJananovich.
Film:	*2081* DVD (30 mins) 2009, short film by IZZIT, Erie, PA.

Harrison Bergeron

Kurt Vonnegut

The year was 2081, and everybody was finally equal. They weren't only equal before God and the law. They were equal every which way. Nobody was smarter than anybody else. Nobody was better looking than anybody else. Nobody was stronger or quicker than anybody else. All this equality was due to the 211th, 212th, and 213th Amendments to the Constitution, and to the unceasing vigilance of agents of the United States Handicapper General.

Some things about living still weren't quite right, though. April for instance, still drove people crazy by not being springtime. And it was in that clammy month that the H-G men took George and Hazel Bergeron's fourteen-year-old son, Harrison, away.

It was tragic, all right, but George and Hazel couldn't think about it very hard. Hazel had a perfectly average intelligence, which meant she couldn't think about anything except in short bursts. And George, while his intelligence was way above normal, had a little mental handicap radio in his ear. He was required by law to wear it at all times. It was tuned to a government transmitter. Every twenty seconds or so, the transmitter would send out some sharp noise to keep people like George from taking unfair advantage of their brains.

George and Hazel were watching television. There were tears on Hazel's cheeks, but she'd forgotten for the moment what they were about.

On the television screen were ballerinas.

A buzzer sounded in George's head. His thoughts fled in panic, like bandits from a burglar alarm.

"That was a real pretty dance, that dance they just did," said Hazel.

"Huh" said George.

"That dance—it was nice," said Hazel.

"Yup," said George. He tried to think a little about the ballerinas. They weren't really very good—no better than anybody else would have been, anyway. They were burdened with sash weights and bags of birdshot, and their faces were masked, so that no one, seeing a free and graceful gesture or a pretty face, would feel like something the cat drug in. George was toying with the vague notion that maybe dancers shouldn't be handicapped. But he didn't get very far with it before another noise in his ear radio scattered his thoughts.

George winced. So did two out of the eight ballerinas.

Hazel saw him wince. Having no mental handicap herself, she had to ask George what the latest sound had been.

"Sounded like somebody hitting a milk bottle with a ball peen hammer," said George.

"I'd think it would be real interesting, hearing all the different sounds," said Hazel a little envious. "All the things they think up.

"Um," said George.

"Only, if I was Handicapper General, you know what I would do?" said Hazel. Hazel, as a matter of fact, bore a strong resemblance to the Handicapper General, a woman named Diana Moon Glampers. "If I was Diana Moon Glampers," said Hazel, "I'd have chimes on Sunday—just chimes. Kind of in honor of religion."

"I could think, if it was just chimes," said George.

"Well—maybe make 'em real loud," said Hazel. "I think I'd make a good Handicapper General."

"Good as anybody else," said George.

"Who knows better than I do what normal is?" said Hazel.

"Right," said George. He began to think glimmeringly about his abnormal son who was now in jail, about Harrison but a twenty-one-gun salute in his head stopped that.

"Boy!" said Hazel, "that was a doozy, wasn't it?"

It was such a doozy that George was white and trembling, and tears stood on the rims of his red eyes. Two of the eight ballerinas had collapsed to the studio floor, were holding their temples.

"All of a sudden you look so tired," said Hazel. "Why don't you stretch out on the sofa, so's you can rest your handicap bag on the pillows, honeybunch." She was referring to the forty-seven pounds of birdshot in a canvas bag, which was padlocked around George's neck. "Go on and rest the bag for a little while," she said. "I don't care if you're not equal to me for a while."

George weighed the bag with his hands. "I don't mind it," he said. "I don't notice it any more. It's just a part of me."

"You been so tired lately—kind of wore out," said Hazel. "If there was just some way we could make a little hole in the bottom of the bag, and just take out a few of them lead balls. Just a few."

"Two years in prison and two thousand dollars fine for every ball I took out," said George. "I don't call that a bargain."

"If you could just take a few out when you came home from work," said Hazel.

"I mean—you don't compete with anybody around here. You just set around."

"If I tried to get away with it," said George, "then other people'd get away with it—and pretty soon we'd be right back to the dark ages again, with everybody competing against everybody else. You wouldn't like that, would you?"

"I'd hate it," said Hazel.

"There you are," said George. The minute people start cheating on laws, what do you think happens to society?"

If Hazel hadn't been able to come up with an answer to this question, George couldn't have supplied one. A siren was going off in his head.

"Reckon it'd fall all apart," said Hazel.

"What would?" said George blankly.

"Society," said Hazel uncertainly. "Wasn't that what you just said?

"Who knows?" said George.

The television program was suddenly interrupted for a news bulletin. It wasn't clear at first as to what the bulletin was about, since the announcer, like all announcers, had a serious speech impediment. For about half a minute, and in a state of high excitement, the announcer tried to say, "Ladies and Gentlemen."

He finally gave up, handed the bulletin to a ballerina to read.

"That's all right—" Hazel said of the announcer, "he tried. That's the big thing. He tried to do the best he could with what God gave him. He should get a nice raise for trying so hard."

"Ladies and Gentlemen," said the ballerina, reading the bulletin. She must have been extraordinarily beautiful, because the mask she wore was hideous. And it was easy to see that she was the strongest and most graceful of all the dancers, for her handicap bags were as big as those worn by two-hundred pound men.

And she had to apologize at once for her voice, which was a very unfair voice for a woman to use. Her voice was a warm, luminous, timeless melody. "Excuse me—" she said, and she began again, making her voice absolutely uncompetitive.

"Harrison Bergeron, age fourteen," she said in a grackle squawk, "has just escaped from jail, where he was held on suspicion of plotting to overthrow the government. He is a genius and an athlete, is under-handicapped, and should be regarded as extremely dangerous."

A police photograph of Harrison Bergeron was flashed on the screen—upside down, then sideways, upside down again, then right side up. The picture showed the full length of Harrison against a background calibrated in feet and inches. He was exactly seven feet tall.

The rest of Harrison's appearance was Halloween and hardware. Nobody had ever borne heavier handicaps. He had outgrown hindrances faster than the H-G men could think them up. Instead of a little ear radio for a mental handicap, he wore a tremendous pair of earphones, and spectacles with thick wavy lenses. The spectacles were intended to make him not only half blind, but to give him whanging headaches besides.

Scrap metal was hung all over him. Ordinarily, there was a certain symmetry, a military neatness to the handicaps issued to strong people, but Harrison looked like a walking junkyard. In the race of life, Harrison carried three hundred pounds.

And to offset his good looks, the H-G men required that he wear at all times a red rubber ball for a nose, keep his eyebrows shaved off, and cover his even white teeth with black caps at snaggletooth random.

"If you see this boy," said the ballerina, "do not—I repeat, do not—try to reason with him."

There was the shriek of a door being torn from its hinges.

Screams and barking cries of consternation came from the television set. The photograph of Harrison Bergeron on the screen jumped again and again, as though dancing to the tune of an earthquake.

George Bergeron correctly identified the earthquake, and well he might have—for many was the time his own home had danced to the same crashing tune. "My God—" said George, "that must be Harrison!"

The realization was blasted from his mind instantly by the sound of an automobile collision in his head.

When George could open his eyes again, the photograph of Harrison was gone. A living, breathing Harrison filled the screen.

Clanking, clownish, and huge, Harrison stood—in the center of the studio. The knob of the uprooted studio door was still in his hand. Ballerinas, technicians, musicians, and announcers cowered on their knees before him, expecting to die.

"I am the Emperor!" cried Harrison. "Do you hear? I am the Emperor! Everybody must do what I say at once!" He stamped his foot and the studio shook.

"Even as I stand here" he bellowed, "crippled, hobbled, sickened—I am a greater ruler than any man who ever lived! Now watch me become what I can become!"

Harrison tore the straps of his handicap harness like wet tissue paper, tore straps guaranteed to support five thousand pounds.

Harrison's scrap-iron handicaps crashed to the floor.

Harrison thrust his thumbs under the bar of the padlock that secured his head harness. The bar snapped like celery. Harrison smashed his headphones and spectacles against the wall.

He flung away his rubber-ball nose, revealed a man that would have awed Thor, the god of thunder.

"I shall now select my Empress!" he said, looking down on the cowering people. "Let the first woman who dares rise to her feet claim her mate and her throne!"

A moment passed, and then a ballerina arose, swaying like a willow.

Harrison plucked the mental handicap from her ear, snapped off her physical handicaps with marvelous delicacy. Last of all he removed her mask.

She was blindingly beautiful.

"Now—" said Harrison, taking her hand, "shall we show the people the meaning of the word dance? Music!" he commanded.

The musicians scrambled back into their chairs, and Harrison stripped them of their handicaps, too. "Play your best," he told them, "and I'll make you barons and dukes and earls."

The music began. It was normal at first—cheap, silly, false. But Harrison snatched two musicians from their chairs, waved them like batons as he sang the music as he wanted it played. He slammed them back into their chairs.

The music began again and was much improved.

Harrison and his Empress merely listened to the music for a while—listened gravely, as though synchronizing their heartbeats with it.

They shifted their weights to their toes.

Harrison placed his big hands on the girl's tiny waist, letting her sense the weightlessness that would soon be hers.

And then, in an explosion of joy and grace, into the air they sprang!

Not only were the laws of the land abandoned, but the law of gravity and the laws of motion as well.

They reeled, whirled, swiveled, flounced, capered, gamboled, and spun.

They leaped like deer on the moon.

The studio ceiling was thirty feet high, but each leap brought the dancers nearer to it.

It became their obvious intention to kiss the ceiling. They kissed it.

And then, neutralizing gravity with love and pure will, they remained suspended in air inches below the ceiling, and they kissed each other for a long, long time.

It was then that Diana Moon Glampers, the Handicapper General, came into the studio with a double-barreled ten-gauge shotgun. She fired twice, and the Emperor and the Empress were dead before they hit the floor.

Diana Moon Glampers loaded the gun again. She aimed it at the musicians and told them they had ten seconds to get their handicaps back on.

It was then that the Bergerons' television tube burned out.

Hazel turned to comment about the blackout to George. But George had gone out into the kitchen for a can of beer.

George came back in with the beer, paused while a handicap signal shook him up. And then he sat down again. "You been crying," he said to Hazel.

"Yup," she said.

"What about?" he said.

"I forget," she said. "Something real sad on television."

"What was it?" he said.

"It's all kind of mixed up in my mind," said Hazel.

"Forget sad things," said George.

"I always do," said Hazel.

"That's my girl," said George. He winced. There was the sound of a riveting gun in his head.

"Gee—I could tell that one was a doozy," said Hazel.

"You can say that again," said George.

"Gee—" said Hazel, "I could tell that one was a doozy."

"Harrison Bergeron"

PLOT-CHECK QUIZ

Directions: Answer each question in a brief but complete sentence. Do not repeat the question.

1. What two kinds of equality had been achieved in the year 2081?

2. In what two ways had these two kinds of equality been achieved?

3. Why is Harrison such a problem for the authorities of 2081?

4. What kind of handicaps did George have?

5. Why does Harrison's mother, Hazel, have no handicaps?

6. What is George's opinion of the government that handicapped him?

7. How does Harrison revolt against the system of handicaps?

8. Does anyone join Harrison's revolt?

9. Why does Harrison's revolt fail?

10. Do George and Hazel realize what had happened to their son at the story's end?

Three Kinds of Questions

"HARRISON BERGERON"
EXERCISE 1

Directions: First, answer each question briefly in the space beneath it. Second, to the left, identify the type of each question: print FACT for factual, INT for interpretation, and EVAL for evaluation.

1. Why does Vonnegut begin the story by making a distinction between equality before God and law and equality "every which way"?
2. How is equality "every which way" maintained in 2081?
3. Why is competition regarded as unfair in 2081?
4. What kind of ruler and government does Harrison want in 2081?
5. Although everyone is unique in America, in what ways are we also equal?
6. Why does Hazel think that people should be rewarded just for trying really hard?
7. Although George's intelligence is way above normal, why does he still defend the government that handicaps him?
8. Should unqualified people be hired for a job?
9. How does the narrator describe what "normal" is?
10. At the end of the story, do Harrison's parents realize what happened to their son?

Qualities of Good Discussion Questions

"HARRISON BERGERON" EXERCISE 2

Directions: At the left of each question, mark GOOD if it has the qualities of a good discussion question. If the question lacks one of the needed qualities, mark it:

NC if the question is NOT CLEAR.
NS if the question is NOT SPECIFIC and could be asked of any story.
LD for LACKS DOUBT because it cannot be answered in more than one way.
NI for NOT INTERPRETIVE because it is factual or evaluation.
NA if it is NOT ANSWERABLE on the basis of the text alone.

1. What is the role of Hazel in the story?
2. Is Vonnegut being sarcastic about everyone being equal in 2081?
3. Why does Harrison's revolt fail?
4. Why does Vonnegut have Harrison's revolt fail?
5. Is Vonnegut using George?
6. Should people be rewarded for trying really hard to do something?
7. Were Hazel and George arrested for their son's revolt against the government?
8. Does Vonnegut want us to regard Harrison as a danger to society?
9. Why is Harrison such an idiot?
10. Why does the government promote mediocrity but not excellence?
11. Why is George preoccupied with faulty technology?
12. Should it be easier to amend the U.S. Constitution?
13. What is Vonnegut saying about the future of our society?
14. How did the Handicapper General get her job?
15. Why does the narrator tell us that by 2081 equality "every which way" has been achieved by Amendments 211, 212, and 213?

Socratic Seminar

"Harrison Bergeron"

Basic Question 1: According to Vonnegut's story, is the desire to excel as strong as the tendency to be mediocre?

If yes, then:

1. Why does Hazel consider herself an authority on what is "normal"? (page 11)

2. Why does George defend the system that handicaps him even though his intelligence is "way above normal"? (12)
3. Why is competition a dirty word in the world of 2081? (12)
4. Why does the playing of the musicians improve only after Harrison physically threatens them? (16)
5. Why does only one person join Harrison's revolt? (15)
6. Why does Vonnegut have Harrison's revolt fail? (17)
7. Does Vonnegut want us to conclude that people like Harrison are as much a danger to society as are people like Hazel and George? (13, 15)

If no, then:

8. Why is the Government of 2081 concerned more with maintaining mediocrity than with encouraging excellence? (10)
9. Why is the "unceasing vigilance" of the Handicapper General's agents needed to maintain equality "every which way"? (10)
10. Why are the penalties for removing a handicap so severe? (12)
11. Why is everyone cautioned not to try to reason with Harrison? (13)
12. Why does the author have a ballerina voluntarily join Harrison's revolt? (15)
13. Why does Vonnegut have Harrison defy not only civil laws but also the laws of gravity and motion? (16)
14. Why does the story end with the Handicapper General back in charge? (17)
15. Do George and Hazel realize what had happened to their son at the story's end?

Basic Question 2: Why does Vonnegut regard a movement toward total equality as a threat to our society?

1. Why does Vonnegut begin the story by making a distinction between equality before God and the law and equality "every which way"?
2. Why does the author tell us that complete equality was achieved in 2081 by the passage of three Amendments as well as by the "unceasing vigilance of agents of the Handicapper General"?
3. Does Vonnegut make the H-G a woman because women, more than men, would likely advocate complete equality?
4. In 2081 where everyone is equal "every which way," why is "normal" described as "cheap, silly, false"?

5. Why does George defend the system that handicaps him?
6. Why does the government use an ear phone to keep George from taking "unfair advantage" of his intelligence?
7. In 2081, why is competition unfair?
8. Why does Hazel think people should be rewarded for effort—for trying really hard?
9. In 2081 why is television so ubiquitous?
10. Why does the government want to control the weight and physical appearance of its citizens.
11. Why is the government of 2081 concerned more with promoting mediocrity than excellence?
12. In 2081, why does it take a dictatorship to maintain "equality every which way"?
13. Why are unqualified people chosen for jobs in 2081.
14. Why does Hazel regard herself as an expert on what is "normal"?

2081: DVD (30 mins) 2009

Of the four movie versions of his story, Vonnegut approves only the 2006 version: "I am glad to see the appropriate measure have been taken with my story." Nevertheless, some critics prefer the 2009 version, *2081* DVD which follows rather closely Vonnegut's original story. However, it makes several radical plot changes which Vonnegut would not likely approve.

Pre-discussion Assignment: View the 30-minute movie twice while making notes on your copy of the text of "Harrison Bergeron." Then, following the Film Guidelines (page 162), write at least ten differences between the two stories. From your list of ten differences, select the three most important and rank them (most to least) for discussion.

Basic Question 3: Would Vonnegut still approve the 2009 version of his "Harrison Bergeron" story even though it makes several plot changes?

If yes, then:

1. Why does the movie begin with an introduction which deplores a world in which there are no heroes?
2. Why does the movie fail to raise the issue whether the desire to excel is as strong as the tendency to be mediocre?
3. In the movie, why does Harrison address the entire audience but only the orchestra in Vonnegut's story?
4. Why does the movie imply that George momentarily recognizes his son, as he smiles at his son when Harrison addresses his audience.

If no, then:

5. Why does the movie follow closely the majority of the plot of Vonnegut's original story?
6. Why is Hazel portrayed as a model of mediocrity who needs no handicaps?
7. Why is Diana Moon Glamper's atrocious summary execution of Harrison broadcast for all to see?
8. Is the failure of Harrison's revolt in the movie more complete than the short story?

Nonfiction Readings

Mediocrity vs. Excellence: "Join the 1% Mindset"

Coach Dayne (September 5, 2013)

There seems to be an acceptance of mediocrity in today's young people. They're being taught to play it safe, in order to hide from disappointment and loss of confidence. Unfortunately, what's not understood strongly enough is the importance of failure and setbacks. Learning to embrace struggle, and fight through pain is an invaluable skill set that needs to be taught to our children. Instead of sheltering them from disappointment, allow them to raise their expectations, risk falling, and learn how to battle through pain. In the long run, they will gain even *more* confidence, knowing that defeat is temporary, and can't stop them!

Coach Stewart of D.R.E.A.M.* Team Athletics recently sent this comparison–contrast list to me, via Twitter. She's an amazing basketball coach and role model, with an intense passion for teaching leadership and eliminating the victim's mentality, on and off the court.

Coach Dayne:

If you want to promote mediocrity in a child, emphasize:	If you want to promote excellence in a child, emphasize:
Comforts	Challenges
Appearance	Substance
Abilities	Accomplishments (help the child to see what s/he can do)
Self-esteem	Self-reliance
Ease	Hard work (discipline)
Self-pity	Responsibility
Immediate gratification	Delayed gratification
Fun	Joy of life-long learning

*Discipline, Respect, Effort, Attitude, Mentality: "Being realistic is the most common path to mediocrity."

Basic Question 4: Why do both coaches, Dayne and Stewart, believe that the desire to excel as not as strong today as the tendency to be mediocre?

The Age of Distraction: Digital Deficit Disorder

"Our life is frittered away by detail."

Henry David Thoreau

"Our infinite capacity for distraction."

Aldous Huxley

We live in curious times. It's called the Age of Information, but in another light it can be called the Age of Distraction.

While humanity has never been free of distraction—from swatting those bothersome gnats around the fireplace to dealing with piles of paper mail and ringing telephones—never have the distractions been so voluminous, so overwhelming, so intense, so persistent as they are now. Ringing phones are one thing, but email notifications, Twitter and Facebook messages, an array of browser tabs open, and mobile devices that are always on and always beeping are quite another. More and more, we are connected, we are up to our necks in the stream of information, we are in the crossfire of the battle for our attention, and we are engaged in a harrying blur of multitasking activity.

When we're working, we have distractions coming from every direction. In front of us is the computer, with email notifications and other notifications of all kinds. Then there's the addicting lure of the browser, which contains not only an endless amount of reading material that can be a black hole into which we never escape, but unlimited opportunities for shopping, for chatting with other people, for gossip and news and lurid photos and so much more. All the while, several new emails have come in, waiting for a quick response. Several programs are open at once, each of them with tasks to complete. Several people would like to chat, dividing our attention even further.

And that's just in front of us. From the sides come a ringing desk phone, a ringing mobile device, music from several different coworkers, a colleague coming to our desk asking a question, incoming papers needing attention, other papers scattered across our desks, someone calling a meeting, another offering up food.

With so much competing for our attention, and so little time to focus on real work, it's a wonder we get anything done at all.

And then we leave work, but the attack on our attention doesn't end. We bring the mobile device, with incoming text and email messages, all needing a reply, with incoming calls that can't be ignored. We have reading material, either in paper form or on the mobile device, to keep our attention occupied. We are bombarded from all sides by advertising, asking for not only attention but our desires. We get home, and there's the television, constantly blaring, with 500 channels all asking for yet more attention, with 500,000 ads asking for yet more desires. There's our home computer, asking us to do more work, sending us more messages, more distractions, social networks and shopping and reading. There are kids or spouses or roommates or friends, there's the home phone, and still the mobile device is going off.

This is unprecedented, and it's alarming.

We've come into this Age without being aware that it was happening, or realizing its consequences. Sure, we knew that the Internet was proliferating, and we were excited about that. We knew that mobile devices were becoming more and more ubiquitous, and maybe some people harrumphed and others welcomed the connectivity. But while the opportunities offered by this online world are a good thing, the constant distractions, the increasingly urgent pull on our attention, the stress of multitasking at an ever-finer granular level, the erosion of our free time and our ability to live with a modicum of peace . . . perhaps we didn't realize how much this would change our lives. Maybe some did. And maybe many still don't realize it. I think, with so many things asking for our attention, it's time we paid attention to this.

It's an Addiction

There's instant positive feedback to such constant activities as checking email, surfing the web, checking social networks such as blogs, forums, Twitter and Facebook. That's why it's so easy to become addicted to being connected and distracted.

Other addictive activities, such as doing drugs or eating junk food, have the same kind of instant positive feedback—you do the activity, and right away, you're rewarded with something pleasurable but don't feel the negative consequences until much later. Checking email, or any similar online activity, has that addictive quality of instant positive feedback and delayed negative feedback.

You check your email and hey! A new email from a friend! You get a positive feeling, perhaps a validation of your self-worth, when you receive a new email. It feels good to get a message from someone. And thus the instant positive feedback rewards you checking email, more and more frequently, until the addiction is solidly ingrained.

Now, you might later get tired of answering all your email, because it's overwhelming and difficult to keep up with. But usually by then, you're addicted and can't stop checking. And usually the checking of the email has positive reward (a good feeling) but it's the activity of answering all the emails that isn't as fun.

It's a New Lifestyle: What Are the Consequences?

Being connected, getting information all the time, having constant distractions . . . it has all become a part of our lives.

Computers, at one time, were a small part of our lives; perhaps we used them at work, but in the car and on the train, and usually at home and when we were out doing other things, we were disconnected. Even at work, our computers had limited capabilities—we could only do certain things with desktop applications, and while solitaire was definitely addicting, it didn't take up your entire life. Not so anymore.

Computers are taking over our lives. And while I'm as pro-technology as the next guy, I also think we need to consider the consequences of this new lifestyle.

Because we've created a new lifestyle very rapidly, and I'm not sure we're prepared for it. We don't have new strategies for dealing with being connected most of the time, we don't have new cultural norms, nor have we figured out if this is the best way to live life. We've been plunged into it, before we could develop a system for handling it.

It's an Expectation

Let's say you woke up one day and decided you no longer wanted to participate in the Age of Distraction in some way . . . could you just drop out? Well, you could, but you'd be up against an entire culture that expects you to participate.

A good example was when I recently announced that I was ditching email so that I could focus less on answering emails and more on what I love doing: creating. That seemed fairly straightforward to me, but it turns out it drew quite a strong reaction in a lot of people. Some applauded me for having the courage to give up email—indicating this was a huge step that took bravery, took an ability to break from a major societal norm. Other people were insulted or indignant, either feeling like I was insulting their way of doing things, or that I was some kind of prima donna or "diva" for not wanting to be available through email.

Interesting: the simple act of giving up email was either hugely courageous, or arrogant, because I wasn't living up to the expectations of society that I'd be available via email and at least make the attempt to reply. Interesting, because just a decade earlier, many people didn't use email and no one cared if they didn't. And email is just one facet of these expectations. How high these expectations are depends on your job, who you are, where you work, and the standards that evolved in your work group. But some people are expected to be available all the time, carrying a Blackberry or other device with them, and to respond almost immediately—or they're out of touch, or not good businesspeople. Others are expected to be available for instant messaging or Skype chats, or be on social forums or social networks such as Facebook or Twitter.

Being connected all the time, being part of this constant stream of distraction, is an expectation that society now has of us. And going against that expectation is immensely difficult for many people—it requires courage, or a willingness to be an arrogant prima donna.

How did this happen? When did we opt in to be a part of this? There was never a time when we agreed to these expectations, but they've evolved rapidly over the last decade or so, and now it's hard to get out. I'm not saying we should get out. I'm saying we need to rethink things, to change expectations so that the system suits us, not the other way around.

An Experiment: An e-media Fast

A colleague requires her students to go on an "e-media fast." For 24 hours, each student must refrain from electronic media. When she announces the assignment, she told me, 90% of the students shrug, thinking it's no big deal. But when they realize all the things they must give up for a whole day—cell phone, computer, Internet, TV, car radio, Facebook, Twitter, Blackberry, iPad, Kindle, etc.—"they start to moan and groan." She tells them they can still read books in print. She acknowledges it will be a tough day, though for roughly 8 of the 24 hours they'll be asleep. She says if they break the fast—if they answer the phone, say, or simply check email—they must begin from scratch.

The Follow-up: A Report

"The papers I get back are amazing," says the professor. "They have titles like 'The Worst Day of My Life' or 'The Best Experience I Ever Had,' always extreme. I thought I was going to die, they'll write. I went to turn on the TV but if I did I realized, my God, I'd have to start all over again. Each student has his or her own weakness—for some it's TV, some the cell phone, some the Internet or their games console. But no matter how much they hate abstaining, or how hard it is to hear the phone ring and not answer it, they take time to do things they haven't done in years.

They actually walked down the street to visit their friend, played a board game, spoke to their parents at length about what they did before the electronic devices, built a model airplane, or made a German chocolate cake. One wrote, 'I thought to do things I hadn't thought to do ever.' The experience changes them. Some are so affected that they determine to fast on their own, one day a month."

On Writing a Commentary: Guidelines

1. Copy the quotation or thesis verbatim.
2. Paraphrase it.
3. Make up a **list of questions** raised by the quotation.
4. Respond in a one-page essay; begin with **a thesis** that agrees or disagrees with the quotation.
   - **Illustrate** with example(s) from literature, history, current events, science, or your own observation or personal experience.
   - **Incorporate** some of the most important questions raised by the quotation in your response (commentary).

Example

1. "Someone has said that success in life is measured not by how far we go but by the direction we choose."
2. "Success depends not on how much we achieve but on the goals that we pursue." Another paraphrase: "Goals are the standard of success, not achievement."
3. Questions raised by the quotation:
   - Success in whose eyes? Mine or those of others?
   - Must success include happiness?
   - Must the direction chosen be honorable and ethical?
   - Why does the quotation center on the metaphor of a journey?
4. Thesis: If the anonymous author of the quotation means that success depends not on how much we achieve but on the goals that we pursue, I disagree for three reasons.

Journal Assignment

Write a Commentary on Shakespeare's quotation:

"Some are born great, some achieve greatness, and some have greatness thrust upon them." (*Twelfth Night* 2.5.145)

1. Copy the quotation or thesis verbatim.
2. Paraphrase it.
3. Make up a list of questions raised by the quotation.
   - What is a synonym for greatness?
   - How does *TIME* magazine define greatness?
   - How does *TIME* select "The Person of the Year"?
   - Why did *TIME* select Albert Einstein and "The Person of the Century"?
   - Was Einstein born great? Did he achieve greatness or have it thrust upon him?
   - What does greatness have to do with excellence in Vonnegut's story?
4. Respond in a one-page essay; begin with a thesis that agrees or disagrees with the quotation.

CHAPTER

13 Lesson Plans 11 and 12

Who Are Your Real Friends?

Lesson Plan 11: *Because of Winn Dixie*

1.	**Focus:**	Journal: What is your definition of a friend? Do you agree with Emerson that "The only way to have a friend is to be one"?
2.	**Objective:**	To review the Three Kinds of Questions and the Qualities of Good Discussion Questions.
3.	**Purpose:**	To develop the habits of independent, reflective, and critical thinking.
4.	**Input:**	Which of the signs of a real friend apply to the characters in *Because of Winn Dixie?*
5.	**Modeling:**	Write ten interpretive questions on *Because of Winn Dixie* (DVD).
6.	**Checking for understanding:**	Co-leaders ask spontaneous follow-up questions of clarification, substantiation, more opinion, consistency, implication, or resolution.
7.	**Guided practice:**	Co-leaders observe the Four Rules of Socratic Discussion.
8.	**Closure and evaluation:**	Essay exam, oral resolution, or written resolution to one of the basic questions.
	Text:	Kate DiCamillo (2001) *Because of Winn-Dixie.* Somervialle MA: Candlewick Press.
	Film:	*Because of Winn-Dixie* DVD (110 mins) 2005.
	Setting:	Naomi, Florida, 1995 (Mr. Alfred refers to eBay).

Characters:

India Opal Buloni—the ten-year-old narrator whose mother had abandoned her family seven years ago.

Winn-Dixie—the stray, "Less Fortunate," dog that Opal befriends.

Pastor Buloni—Opal's father (who has no first name); he is pastor of Open Arms Baptist Church and loves his daughter dearly.

Mr. Alfred—manager of Friendly Corners Trailer Park. See the Movie Critic's sheet.

Miss Fanny Block—the librarian of the Merman W. Block Memorial Library.

Gloria Dump—a near-blind black woman whom the Dunlap brothers regard as the neighborhood witch.

Otis—the shy ex-con clerk at Gertrude's Pets Store who sings to the animals and gives Opal a job.

Dunlap (10) and Steve (9) Dewberry—neighborhood brothers who harass Opal.

Amanda Wilkinson—a peer of Opal whose five-year-old brother, Carson, had drowned.

Sweetie Pie Thomas—a five-year-old who desperately wants to have her own dog.

Because of Winn Dixie

PLOT-CHECK QUIZ

Directions: On your own paper, answer each question briefly in the space beneath it and then identify the type of each question: print FACT for factual, INT for interpretation, and EVAL for evaluation.

1. How does India Opal Buloni happen to find Winn-Dixie?

2. How does Opal get her father to allow her to keep Winn-Dixie?

3. What is one of the ten important things that her father tells Opal about her mama?

4. Why does Opal speak so often about her mama?

5. Why does her father allow Opal to bring her dog into the church?

6. After Winn-Dixie interrupts the sermon, for whom does Opal's father ask his congregation to pray?

7. After her father's sermon, what does Opal tell God?

8. Who becomes Opal's first true friend?

9. How does Opal become friends with the person in question 8?

10. Why does Opal go to Gertrude's Pet Store?

11. After her first visit to Gertrude's store, why is Opal suddenly happy?

12. How does Opal happen to meet Gloria Dump?

13. How can Gloria Dump see Opal with her heart?

14. Based on what you know about Opal in the first nine chapters, would you want to become her friend? If so, how would you go about it? If not, why not?

15. Is God important in your life?

Review Quiz: Qualities of Good Discussion Questions

Directions: On your own paper, mark GOOD if a question would lead to a disagreement based on the book. If the question lacks one of the needed qualities, mark it:
NC if the question is NOT CLEAR.
NS if the question is NOT SPECIFIC and could be asked of any story.
LD for LACKS DOUBT since it cannot be answered in more than one way.
FACT for FACTUAL and cannot be discussed.
EVAL for EVALUATION that could be answered without reading the story.

1. What kind of relationship do Opal and her father have?
2. After her father allows Opal to keep Winn-Dixie, why does he say the dog would be trouble?
3. What is the role of Otis in the story?
4. What if this was a real story and she was only dreaming?
5. Did Opal's father really love her mother?
6. Why does Otis give Opal a job at Gertrude's Pet Store?
7. Do the Dewberry brothers believe that Gloria is a witch?
8. What is the story saying about kids who think they're always right?
9. Why does Opal memorize the list of ten things her father told her about her mama?
10. What does the title of the story mean?
11. Although Opal loves her father, why does she repeatedly describe him as a turtle?
12. Does Opal ever find out why Amanda is so stuck up?
13. Why does he just let her go like that?
14. Why does Opal suggest that she and her dog be Miss Fanny's friends?
15. What does the bear in the library have to do with Opal's dog?

Socratic Seminar

Basic Question 1: What is "the important thing" about life that Opal learns "because of Winn-Dixie"? (page 60)

1. Why does Gloria Dump think "the most important thing" is something different for everyone? (page 96)
2. By the end of the story, what "complicated and wonderful gifts" has Opal discovered in her friends? (153)
3. How does Opal finally learn to accept the fact that her mama will never return? (178)
4. At the end of the story, why is Opal's heart no longer empty over the loss of her mother? (178)
5. By the end of the story, has Opal's or her father's life changed more?
6. What does Opal mean when she says "Just about everything that happened to me that summer happened to me because of Winn-Dixie"? (60)
7. In the last chapter, why does the author have Opal examine her tree in Gloria Dump's yard? (69 and 178)
8. Why does Opal wonder if she seemed like a ghost to her mama or her mama just sometimes seemed like a ghost to her? (97)
9. When Opal prayerfully speaks to her mother, why does she speak of her *father* finally realizing that her mother will not be retuning? (178)

Basic Question 2: Would the author agree with the plot changes in the movie?

If so, why so? If not, why not?

Although the film is 95 percent true to the Kate DiCamillo's story, so much so that there can be no question she would approve it, there are four notable differences that make us wonder if the author would regard these changes as major or minor and if she would regard them as improvements or distortions of her story.

1. The film opens with Opal pretending to play baseball with herself. Does this scene set the tone for the story?
2. Mr. Alfred, manager of Friendly Corners Trailer Park, becomes an important minor character who gives Opal's father a special rate out of deference to the church but will not allow Opal to keep a dog. Mr. Alfred demands that the preacher calls the pound to remove Winn-Dixie because Opal's father did not get rid of him as promised. In a moment of crisis, the preacher has to side with Opal to keep the dog and to eventually convince Mr. Alfred to agree. His reference to getting quotations on eBay for selling a dog date

the film (circa 1995). Mr. Alfred also appears in the concluding scene of the party at Gloria Dump's home. He completes the picture of how Winn-Dixie had brought together such a disparate group of people.

Question: Why is Mr. Alfred developed into an important minor character?

3. The film adds a police officer who appears in two scenes. At first he goes to Gertrude's Pets store to hassle Otis about his criminal record. In the second scene he becomes a stereotype of the bumbling cop who disrupts a ball game that Winn-Dixie cuts short because he catches the ball and runs away with it.

Question: Why has a policeman been added to the movie version of DiCamillo's novel?

4. The film moves the preacher's prayer before the food is served at Gloria and Opal's party to the closing scene when everyone sings hymns together. At this point, the theme of friendship becomes explicit: "Dear God, we thank you most of all for friends. We appreciate the complicated and wonderful gifts you give us in each other. And we appreciate the task you put down before us, of loving each other the best we can, even as you love us.

Question: Why does the movie end with the preacher's prayer unlike the movie which ends with Miss Fanny offering Opal a Littmus Lozenge?

Note: The greatest single similarity is Opal's seven-year obsession with her mother's absence. More than twenty times, Opal speaks explicitly about her mother. So many references (pages 21, 29, 30, 38, 43, 50, 57, 67, 68, 85, 95, 97, 115, 127, 132, 136, 145, 163, 165, 167, and 177) lead to a basic question of interpretation:

How does Opal finally learn to accept the truth that he mama will never return?

Lesson Plan 12: Who Are Your Real Friends?: Jean Stafford, "Bad Characters"

1. **Focus:** Journal: Have your parents ever told you to stay away from "bad characters?" If so, who did they have in mind? If not, ask your parents to tell you who they regard as "bad characters"? (Alternative topics: (1) Have you ever stolen anything of value? Why? How did you feel? Did you get caught? If not, did you continue stealing?; (2) What is worse than stealing? Why? What is not as bad as stealing? Why?; (3) Have you ever been caught stealing or doing something

illegal? If so, how did you feel? What did you say? How did you react?; (4) Have you ever had a friend who you discovered was doing something really wrong? If so, what did you do? Why?)

2. Objective:	To review the Three Kinds of Questions and the Qualities of Good Discussion Questions.
3. Purpose:	To develop the habits of independent, reflective, and critical thinking.
4. Input:	Review the six qualities of good interpretive questions.
5. Modeling:	Write ten interpretive questions on "Bad Characters." Include a page reference for each.
6. Checking for understanding:	Co-leaders ask spontaneous follow-up questions of clarification, substantiation, more opinion, consistency, implication, or resolution.
7. Guided practice:	Co-leaders observe the Four Rules of Socratic Discussion.
8. Closure and evaluation:	Essay exam, oral resolution, or written resolution to one of the basic questions.
Text:	Jean Stafford (1981) "Bad Characters," *Short Stories: Characters in Conflict* (John Warriner, Ed.). Chicago IL: Harcourt Brace Jovanovich (pages 260–282). Available for free download from *The New Yorker* at http://tinyurl.com/px4znyl, so you can easily print it for classroom use.
Setting:	Adams, Colorado, 1940s.

Characters:

Mr. Vanderpool—Emily's father who loves Emily dearly and enjoys her sense of humor.

Mrs. Vanderpool—Emily's mother is preoccupied with the new baby, Tess. After Emily is caught shoplifting with Lottie, Emily says she "cried for days because she had nurtured an outlaw."

Emily Vanderpool—in an introspective moment, Emily says of herself: "I had a bad character, I know that, but my badness never gave me half the enjoyment Jack and Stella thought it did." Emily had a habit of throwing a temper tantrum whenever she needed "to be alone," or when she knew it "gave her an advantage."

Jack Vanderpool—Emily's older brother who unknowingly almost "saw glory" when Emily had a butcher knife in her hand as he kept taunting her as a "Polecat."

Stella Vanderpool—Emily's younger sister, "a prig," who insists on calling Emily "Kitty" because of her devotion to Muff, her cat.

Tess Vanderpool—Emily's newly arrived baby sister.

Lottie Jump—Unlike the upper class wealth of Emily, Lottie Jump (like Emily also age eleven), is poor. She lives in Arapahoe Creek, "in a wretched settlement made up of people so poor and so sick that each time Emily passes there she 'felt a blush of guilt.'" Lottie has spent her life living by her wits. Full of spunk and complete self-confidence, her personality immediately mesmerizes Emily. And yet Emily is revolted by Lottie's stealing.

Judge Bay—a stereotype of the pompous and preachy grown-ups who scold Emily for stealing.

Mr. Bellamy—a floorwalker at Woolworth's who catches Lottie shoplifting and is duped by her deaf-and-dumb act. He even believes that Emily is the real thief.

"Bad Characters"

PLOT-CHECK QUIZ

Directions: On your own paper, answer each question briefly in the space beneath it and then identify the type of each question: print FACT for factual, INT for interpretation, and EVAL for evaluation.

1. How do Emily Vanderpool and Lottie Jump first meet?

2. Why is Emily immediately attracted to and fascinated with Lottie?

3. What is an important difference between where the Vanderpool and Jump families live?

4. How does Emily respond when she first finds out that Lottie thinks stealing is a picnic?

5. After Emily realizes that Lottie is "big trouble," why doesn't she avoid her?

6. Why does Emily betray Lottie in Woolworth's?

7. Why does Lottie betray Emily at the same time?

8. Like Emily, would you have betrayed Lottie?

9. After Emily had been arrested, why does Emily's father take her to Judge Bay?

10. What does Emily learn from her experience with Lottie Jump?

"Bad Characters"

REVIEW QUIZ: QUALITIES OF GOOD DISCUSSION QUESTIONS

Directions: On your own paper, mark GOOD if a question would lead to a discussion based on the story. If the question lacks one of the required qualities, mark it:

NC if the question is NOT CLEAR and would have to be explained.
NS if the question is NOT SPECIFIC and could be asked of any story.
LD for LACKS DOUBT since it cannot be answered in more than one way.
FACT for FACTUAL because it has but one correct answer.
EVAL for EVALUATION since it is not about understanding what happens in the story.

1. What is the author's purpose in writing this story?

2. Does Emily ever see Lottie again?

3. Does Stafford intend her story to be entirely comical and satirical?

4. Do you think the girl thought what was going to happen happened anyway?

5. Have you ever embarrassed your parents by doing something illegal?

6. Was the judge trying to make the girl feel guilty for not going to the police?

7. Does Emily think that Lottie is kinda dumb?

8. What kind of relationship do Emily and Lottie have?

9. Does the deaf-and-dumb act have something to do with a baby?

10. Why is Emily attracted to and repulsed by Lottie?

11. Does Emily forgive Lottie for getting her in trouble?

12. Why does Stafford have Lottie rewarded for stealing but Emily shamed and punished?

13. Like Emily, would you have helped Lottie shoplift?

Socratic Seminar

"Bad Characters" by Jean Stafford

Basic Question 1: Why is Emily Vanderpool fascinated and revolted by Lottie Jump?

1. When she first meets Lottie, why is Emily instantly interested in her? (pages 262–264)
2. Why does Emily promptly befriend Lottie? (266)
3. Why does Emily describe Lottie as "evilly ugly"? (266)
4. Why does Emily feel "brave and lily-livered" when she goes to town with Lottie to steal? (273)
5. After Emily realizes that Lottie is "big Trouble," why doesn't she avoid her? (273)
6. Why is Emily's friendship with Lottie the longest she ever had? (273)
7. For what reason does Emily think Lottie betrays her? (280)
8. Why is Emily not proud to be *seen* with Lottie but proud to *be* with her? (277)
9. What kind of "Somebody" is Emily with Lottie? (277)
10. Why does Emily hate Lottie even today? (281)

Basic Question 2: What is the difference between Emily's "badness" and Lottie's?

1. Why does Emily allow Lottie to steal from her own family? (pages 264, 268–269)
2. Why does Emily think stealing is sinful and unlawful while Lottie regards it as fun and entertainment? (267 and 275)
3. Does Stafford want us to regard Lottie Jump as no more than a petty thief?
4. What does Emily mean when she says that she knows she has a "bad character"? (273)
5. Why does Emily confide in us that her badness never gave her as much enjoyment as Jack and Stella thought it did? (273)
6. Why is Emily not proud to be *seen* with Lottie but proud to *be* with her? (277)
7. Why does Lottie begin to think that the whole "enterprise" of stealing is pointless? (279)
8. Why is Emily relieved that she has no part in the actual stealing but still follow Lottie's directions? (275)

9. Why does Emily mention that Lottie was caught twice stealing? (276, 280)
10. Why does Emily break her friendship with Lottie by telling her she doesn't have any brains? (280)
11. Did Emily plan to have Lottie caught at the dime store?
12. What does Emily mean when she says "if I rooted out all the badness in me there wouldn't be anything left of me"? (282)

Basic Question 3: Does Stafford intend her story to be entirely comical and satirical?

1. What bitter lesson does Emily learn "by experience" as a result of her encounter with Lottie? (260 and 282)
2. Why does Emily describe her dear cat, Muff, as such a pathetic animal? (260–261)
3. Why would Emily "chloroform" baby Tess if she called her Kitty? (261)
4. After she meets Lottie, why does Emily mention that Muff was unaware that Lottie had replaced her? (269)
5. Why does Stafford have Lottie rewarded for stealing but Emily shamed and punished? (280–282)
6. Why does Stafford portray Judge Bay as a pompous scolding adult?
7. After Emily is caught stealing, does Stafford want Emily to take to heart Judge Bay's warning? (282)
8. After her experience with Lottie, why does Emily stop telling off people when she feels the need to be alone? (282)
9. Why does Emily enjoy throwing tantrums? (261, 269)
10. Why does Stafford have Mr. Bellamy and Emily's father duped by Lottie's "affliction"? (281)
11. After Lottie is out of Emily's life, why does she ask the reader a question that she answers herself? ("What's the use of telling you the rest? You know what happened.") (281)
12. Why does the story end with Emily telling us that "It is not true that you don't learn by experience?" (282)
13. Is Emily's correct use of grown-up words meant to be entertaining and humorous?
14. For example, why does Emily boast that by the time she was eight "the most *grandiloquent* gangster could have added nothing to my vocabulary"? (260)

Basic Question 4: Does Stafford give Emily a sophisticated (grown-up) vocabulary because she is telling her story in retrospect (as an adult)?

Rephrased: Does Stafford intend Emily's story to be a vocabulary lesson for middle school students or to imply that eleven-year-old Emily uses correctly grown-up words because she is telling her own story as an adult.

260: scabbards, vilely, pious, prim, grandiloquent, irrevocable, invective, alienated
261: venomous, tantrum, chloroform, mania, bootlegger, euphemism
262: conspicuous, prodigious
265: pathos, cynical, solitary
267: amiable, agitation, prim, monotony
269, 272, 282: polecat
269: weltschmerzlich
270: vexed, infamous, haberdashery
271: pilfers, concentrated, mite
272: stupendous, wrenching, perishing
273: Methuselah, mesmerized
275: insouciant
276: desultory
277: deliberative, floor walker
278: mottled, vexation, pandemonium, giddy, condescending
279: Miss Fagin, enterprise, idiosyncrasy
280: crucial
281: transient, afflicted
282: curmudgeon, declamation, nurtured, hemlocks

Note: The page references are from the edition given in Lesson Plan 12 on page 170.

Suggestion: Before students look up each of these words, *ask them first to figure out from the context* what that word may mean. Model the first fourteen words for your students (*for example*: Does "grandiloquent" (page 260) sound like something good or bad? Why does Emily boast that her vocabulary was beyond that of any gangster?)

Nonfiction Readings

Who Are Your Real Friends?

There are many different kinds of people in your life: school mates, neighbors, acquaintances, strangers—and then there are your friends. But how can you tell who your true friends are? Who are the ones who will see you through thick and thin, the good and the bad, the ups and the downs? Since it is hard to know who your "really real" friends are, here is a list of five ways to tell.

1. *Do they share secrets with you?* It may sound childish, but a true friend sees you as a trustworthy person and shares personal information with you. From what's going on at work to their love life, a true friend doesn't have dark areas of their life that you're not allowed to see. Of course, even more importantly, do you share secrets with them? Do you trust that they will keep what you tell them to themselves? Be on the lookout if they share other people's secrets with you. This is not a good sign that they are keeping your private life private.
2. *Are you able to give them advice?* It's important in a real friendship for friends to be able to give each other feedback on their lives. For example, what would your friend do if you tried to tell her the person she is dating is obviously using her? Would she get angry and storm out? Or would she stop and consider that you have her best interests at heart? Do you feel that the advice they give you comes from that same place of compassion, or does it seem that they are just trying to prove that they know more than you? Real friends just want the best for each other.
3. *A true friend will both admit fault and ask for forgiveness* when he is in the wrong, and extend forgiveness to you when you are in the wrong. Remember, though, that extending or receiving forgiveness doesn't necessarily mean that everything will be perfect between you and back to normal. Trust has to be rebuilt slowly, but a real friend won't continue to bring up your mistakes at every opportunity.
4. *In a real friendship, your friend will stick up for you* whether you are there or not. It's one thing for a friend to tell someone to back off who is yelling at you in public. A true friend will tell someone to stop talking negatively about you even if you aren't there. He will also let you know if someone you think is your friend is saying horrible things about you behind your back, even if it means risking the other person being mad at him. Someone who does not stand up for you is not your friend.
5. *Finally, you can trust a real friend with things you care about.* You can let her be alone with your significant other without worrying. You can loan her personal items without wondering if you'll ever see your things again. You can trust that she will keep your confidence and watch out for you even when you didn't ask her to.

Shoplifting Sacramento County Sheriff's Department

When you and your friends are shopping, do you get irritated or angry because you can only take three pairs of jeans into the dressing room? The ring you wanted to look at is locked in a case? You have to check all your packages at the door? Sales clerks watch you and your friends suspiciously as you look around?

Shoplifting is an expensive problem that everybody pays the price for. It hurts you in several ways—prices keep going up as store owners try to recover some of their losses. A big department store can spend millions a year on security, but it may lose as much as $2,000 a day to shoplifters. And shoplifters give teenagers a bad name.

Who Shoplifts?

- Teens: About 24 percent of apprehended shoplifters are between 13 and 17 years old.
- Amateurs make up the largest number, not professional thieves. These are "everyday" people who steal on impulse, because they see an item they greatly desire, or for a thrill. They tend to believe they won't get caught or sent to jail.
- Most are customers who steal frequently from places where they regularly shop.
- Some are professional thieves who make their living by stealing and selling goods, but this is a much smaller group than the amateurs.
- Drug addicts steal to support their habit.
- Desperate people steal because they need food—but they make up only a very small number of shoplifters.
- Kleptomaniacs, a tiny minority of shoplifters who have a mental disorder that makes it difficult to overcome their urge to steal.

Why Do People Shoplift?

Many want to see if they can get away with it. Some use the excuses, "This is a big store, they can afford it," "I don't have enough money," or "Stores just write it off as a business expense." Many teens shoplift on a dare, thinking their friends will call them "chicken" if they don't go along with the dare. Other teens are just looking for excitement.

Costs for the Individual Teen Who Shoplifts

- When salespeople or security officers catch shoplifters, they call the police, who then arrest the suspects and take them to the police station.

- Children and teens may be released into their parents' custody if it's their first offense.
- The case may be referred to a juvenile office, which can recommend an appropriate punishment, or sent directly to the juvenile court where a judge decides the penalty.
- Everyone will find out about the arrest because police or court officers will interview the shoplifter's parents, neighbors, and school while they're writing the report on the crime.
- If teens are caught shoplifting, their juvenile police records are supposed to be confidential and unavailable to future employers, but sometimes that information does get out.

Costs for Teenagers in General

- They are affected by the higher prices caused by shoplifters. A store owner loses money every time an item is stolen and has to raise prices to compensate for that loss. Store owners also have to spend additional money for special security measures, such as security guards and electronic monitoring.
- There may be fewer jobs available to teens if store owners lose money to shoplifters—owners won't generate enough profit to pay employees.
- Teens who shoplift may also cause problems for their friends and classmates who want to shop or get jobs. Because some store owners see teens as people who are likely to steal, they may not want teens in their stores.
- Teen shoplifting puts a strain on relationships between all other teens and store owners. Some stores have policies that restrict the number of teenagers who can enter the store at one time.
- Some people in the community may hold a negative opinion about teens in general because incidents of teen shoplifting they hear about.

What Happens in Your Community

- Neighborhood store closes because the owner loses too much money to shoplifting. (Thirty percent of business failures in the United States are due to shoplifting and employee theft.)
- A store victimized by shoplifting has to lay off employees because revenue is very low.
- The neighborhood store's customers may have to travel farther to shop after the store closes.
- If the store stays in business, the owner may raise prices to pay for extra security equipment or guards.

Take Action

- If you see anybody in a store take something without paying, report it to a salesperson, security guards, or a cashier. The person is really stealing from you.
- For a class project, interview the security managers of department stores or malls to find out how much shoplifting costs them. Ask about what they do to prevent it.
- Copy and pass out this brochure to teens at your local mall or downtown shopping district.

Source: Sacramento County Sheriff's Department **http://www.sacsheriff.com/pages/crimeprevention/juvenilecrimes02.aspx**

CHAPTER

14 Lesson Plan 13

How Important is God in Your Life?

Judy Blume, *Are You There God? It's Me, Margaret*

1. **Focus:**	Journal: Do you agree with those who believe that a child's religion becomes that of their parents—that a child is born Christian or Jewish or another religion?
2. **Objective:**	To increase our understanding and enjoyment of the story of the importance of God in Maragaret's life.
3. **Purpose:**	To develop the habits of reflective, critical, and independent thinking.
4. **Input:**	Socratic Seminar on three basic interpretive questions.
5. **Modeling:**	Teacher leads the discussion of basic question 1: How do these quotations reveal Margaret's image or idea of God? In what kind of God does Margaret confide?
6. **Checking for understanding:**	Co-leaders ask spontaneous follow-up questions of clarification, substantiation, more opinion, consistency, implication, or resolution.
7. **Guided practice:**	Co-leaders observe the Four Rules of Socratic Discussion.
8. **Closure and evaluation:**	Essay exam, oral resolution, or written resolution to one of the basic questions.
Text:	Judy Blume (1970). *Are You There God? It's Me, Margaret*. New York: Random House Children's Books/Yearling.

Characters:

Margaret Simon—twelve years old, and an only child, who is starting the sixth grade. She's just starting puberty and noticing boys, plus she's uncertain of which religion she prefers to follow.

Barbara Simon (Hutchins)—Margaret's stay-at-home mother, who is Christian.

Herbert Simon—Margaret's father, an insurance salesman, who is Jewish.

Sylvia Simon—Margaret's grandmother and Herbert's mother. She refers to Margaret as "my Margaret" or her "Jewish girl." Her fond hope is that Margaret converts to Judaism.

Nancy Wheeler—Margaret's neighbor and her first new friend in Farbrook, NJ who is also in 6th grade helps Margaret become comfortable in her new environment.

Gretchen Potter—a friend of Nancy whose father is a doctor; she is a member of the Four PTS (Pre-Teen Sensations)—their "secret group."

Janie Loomis—another girl in the Four PTSs with Nancy, Gretchen, and Margaret. She inevitably is the last of the four to get her period.

Evan Wheeler—Nancy's older brother.

Moose Freed—Evan's friend and a boy Margaret gets interested in.

Miles J. Benedict Jr.—Margaret's sixth grade teacher who is in his first year at Margaret's new school, Delano Elementary School.

Laura Danker—classmate of Margaret's ("The big blond with big *you know whats* who has a bad reputation").

Philip Leroy—a classmate of Margaret whom she kisses at a party Spin the Bottle.

Mary and Paul Hutchins—Barbara's estranged parents, who all but disown Barbara for marrying outside her Christian religion.

Are You There God?

PLOT-CHECK QUIZ

1. In school, what year-long individual study project does Margaret choose?

2. Why don't Margaret's parents and grandparents get along?

3. Why does Margaret like and feel comfortable with her Jewish grandmother?

4. Why does Margaret run out of a church in tears after she stumbles into a confessional where an unseen priest asks about her "problems"?

5. What "problem" does Margaret share with three friends in their PTS group?

6. What disturbance at home causes Margaret to stop speaking to God for some time?

7. How does Margaret know when her main growing-up "problem" is solved?

8. What does Margaret do first when she discovers that her period has finally arrived?

9. What does Margaret do when she puts on a pad?

10. What is Margaret's final prayer that Judy Blume uses to end her story?

Socratic Seminar

Basic Question 1: How do these quotations reveal Margaret's image or idea of God? What kind of God does Margaret confide in?

I'm so scared. God. (page 1)
Don't you think it's time for me to start growing, God? (14)
My father doesn't know you the way I do.(16)
Please help me grow, God. (37)
I'm not going to make any decisions without asking you first. (53)
I'm going to temple today. I'll look for you God. (57)
I've been to church. I didn't feel anything special. I'm sure it has nothing to do with You. (63)
I'm really thinking hard God. But I haven't come up with any answers. (76)
See how nice my bra looks now! (82)
Which religion should I be? Sometimes I wish I'd been born one way or the other. (94)
Please God help me! I just want to be normal. (100)
I will wait to find out from you if I am normal or not. (108)
Why God? Why do I feel you only when I'm alone? (120)
Everything's wrong. I've always tried to do what you wanted. Really. (126)
Are you still there God? It's me, Margaret. I know you're there God. I know you wouldn't have missed it for anything! Thank you God. Thanks an awful lot. (149)

Basic Question 2: Does Margaret's God remind you of Viktor Frankl's "operational definition of God" that he found when he was her age?

> God is the partner of our most intimate soliloquies. That is to say, whenever you are talking to yourself in utmost sincerity and ultimate solitude—he to whom you are addressing yourself may justifiably be called God. The irreligious person insists that his soliloquies are just that—monologues with himself and the religious person interprets his as real dialogues with someone other than himself. *I think that what here should count first and more than anything else is the "utmost sincerity" and honesty.* I am sure that if God really exists he certainly is not going to argue with the irreligious persons who mistake him for their own selves and therefore misname him.

Viktor Frankl, *Man's Search for Ultimate Meaning and Man's Search for Meaning*

Note: According to a survey of the Book of the Month Club and the Library of Congress, *Man's Search for Meaning* belongs to a list of "the ten most influential books in the United States." At the time of the author's death at 92 in 1997, the book had sold over 10 million copies and had been translated into 24 languages.

Basic Question 3: Why doesn't Margaret "find" or discover God in a Jewish Temple or a Christian Church?

1. Why is the title a question rather than a greeting?
2. What is Margaret's image or idea of God? (Review Basic Question 1.)
3. Are both grandparents equally intolerant of one another's faith?
4. How would you describe the Jewish and Christian grandparents' concept of faith?
5. What does Margaret mean when she says "I don't think a person can decide to be a certain religious faith. It's like having to choose your own name." (143)
6. What is Margaret thanking God for in her last prayer? (149)
7. Why does Margaret say that if she ever has children, she will "tell them what religion they are so they can start learning about it at an early age"?
8. Why is twelve very late to learn?
9. Do you agree with those agnostic parents who tell their children they will have to decide for themselves what religion, if any, they will embrace?
10. What is the difference between a nominal Christian, Jew, or Muslim and a "True Believer"?

Nonfiction Readings

Why I am Still a Christian

Hans Kung

"Always be ready to give an explanation to anyone who asks for the reason for your hope."

1 Peter 3:15

Where do I get my Christian commitment from? I get my essential values from Jesus of Nazareth, who is a historical figure not a myth, and who is for that very reason the Christ who is authoritative in all things for Christians of all times. He proclaimed the one and only God, his God and our Father (Abba) who had already spoken and been addressed in the history of the people of Israel, in the experiences of men and women; he proclaimed this God with a human face, as living and close. In his whole life and in everything he did he made this face of God shine out. When Jesus spoke of this God and acted in his name, he made clear what was vague in the Old Testament, made what seemed ambiguous there unambiguous. The one true God of Israel is now understood in a new way. We can sum it up by saying that he is understood as the "running Father" (Luke 15:20) of the Prodigal Son, indeed as the Father of all the lost, not simply as the Father of the devout and those who were righteous from the very beginning.

This God as Jesus proclaimed him, is not—as has often been taught to children—an all too masculine, arbitrary, legal-minded God, a kind of martinet, a God without features. He is not a God created in the images of kings, tyrants, and dictators. This God really is—not in its superficial meaning, but in its deepest sense—the loving God who is my Mother too: that is, he is the God of love who for all his justice, commits himself unreservedly to all human beings, in all their needs and hopes.

He is a God who does not always merely demand, but gives; who does not oppress, but liberates; who does not make people ill or poison their lives, but heals them. He is a God who spares those who fall—and who does not fall? A God who forgives instead of condemning, liberates instead of punishing, makes grace rule instead of law; who rejoices more over the repentance of one sinner than over ninety-nine just people. He is therefore a God who prefers the Prodigal Son to the one who stayed home, the tax collector to the Pharisee, the Samaritan heretic to the orthodox, the prostitutes and adulterers to their self-righteous judges. As you see, this preaching of

Jesus was offensive and scandalous, not only for that time in history but for today as well, particularly since it was accompanied by an equally offensive and scandalous practice: not excommunication but communication—even communion! He sat down—he even sat down at table—with the despised and the failures, "sinners" of every kind.

Yes, this God is a different God: a God who sets himself above the formal, logical, merciless correctness of the law and proclaims a "better" righteousness, and may even justify a transgressor of the law; a God for whom the commandments and the Sabbath exist for the sake of the human person, and not the human person for the sake of the commandments and the Sabbath.

It was for this God and his wonderful kindness that Jesus pleaded. For him he spoke, fought, suffered, and was executed. And at this point, of course, the question always arises: did it not all end with his death? The cautious answer can at first be one that even the non-Christian can accept. It is a fact of world history that Jesus' death was not the end of everything but only the beginning; that his first community, in a truly reckless fashion, proclaimed him—the heretical teacher, false prophet, seducer of the people, blasphemer, allegedly condemned by God—to be God's Messiah, the Christ, Lord, Son of man, Son of God. And why? According to the New Testament sources, they were convinced—and only this conviction explains the emergence of Christianity at all—that Jesus had died, not into nothingness, but into God. That means that Jesus is living: living through, with and in God. What for? For us: as hope, as obligation, for our essential values.

Even since then both Christians and non-Christians have been faced with a clear alternative in the direction they lead their lives.

There is the possibility that we die into nothingness. I would not deny my respect for anyone who adopts this position. This is the view which sometimes demands heroism, and can certainly not be refuted. Of course no one has proved it positively either. There has never yet been anyone who could prove that we die into nothingness, that all our living, laboring, loving and suffering ends in nothingness and was ultimately for nothing. And to me this possibility does not seem reasonable; under no circumstances does it seem reasonable.

This is the other possibility: that we die into an absolute reality which we call God, because we still have no better name for it. This alternative too cannot be proved; nor of course can it be refuted. Here every human being is faced with a decision that no one can take away. We have no rational proof for eternal life. But we do have reasonable grounds. We can commit ourselves to this in enlightened, reasonable trust. Truly, not to console ourselves with the promise of a hereafter, but to set ourselves all the more decisively in the here and now, in this life, in this present-day society. And that we do not die into nothingness but into God seems to me more reasonable. Think: if God really exists and if he really is God, he cannot be merely the god of the beginning, but must also be the God of the end. Then he is our Finisher as well as our Creator. And it is he alone, the Creator and Preserver of the cosmos and of human beings, who can be expected to have one more word to say, even in dying at death, beyond the frontiers of all that has hitherto been experienced: to have the last word, just as he had the first. If I seriously believe in an eternal living God, I believe also in God's eternal life, in my own eternal life. So if I begin my profession of faith in the Creed with belief in God the almighty, the creator I may very well finish it with belief in "life everlasting."

A firm faith of this kind changes even this present life completely. It enables us to live quite differently, with more meaning, more responsibility, with greater involvement. In fact it enables us to live in accordance with the standard of this Christ. With his proclamation, the way he lived, and his fate. He became the standard for those who believe in him: the standard for their relations with their fellow human beings, with society, and above all with God. To put it briefly, for believers the true man Jesus of Nazareth has therefore always been the real and clear revelation of the one God: his Messiah, his Christ, his image and his son.

But it is in this very way that he is truly a human being, *the* true human being. Through his proclamation, his behavior, his whole destiny, he provided *a model of being human* which, if we commit ourselves trustingly to it, enables us again and again to discover and to realize the meaning of our own being human, of our freedom, of our life: in our own existence and in living with our fellow human beings. Confirmed by God in the resurrection, he thus represents for us the enduring, reliable, ultimate standard of what being human means. What has surely become plain in recent theological disputes is that Christology, or a theory about Christ, may be important, particularly for theologians and bishops, but faith in Christ and discipleship are the essentials. Being a Christian is the important thing. And it is he who makes that possible for me—he the Christ of God, who is identical with the historical human being who lived, died, and rose again—the Jesus of Nazareth, the devout Galilean Jew of the first third of the first century. So that is how I answer the question of why I am still a Christian and where I get my Christian commitment from.

Why I Am a Jew

Debbie Friedman

Singer and songwriter Debbie Friedman, who died January 9, 2011 of pneumonia, wrote this letter to Daniel Pearl, the Wall Street Journal *reporter who was murdered in 2002 on assignment in Pakistan. In it she expresses her own deep connection to her faith. It was published in the 2005 anthology* I Am Jewish: Personal Reflections Inspired by the Last Words of Daniel Pearl, *and is republished here with permission by Jewish Lights, the publisher.*

Dear Daniel,

This is the first time I have had to think about the "why" of the words "I am a Jew." I have never defined myself or my work before I was born into a Jewish family, exposed to Jewish experiences and Jewish people.

The concept "I am a Jew" never crossed my mind until I was asked to reflect on your words.

I actually chose to be who I am. I felt that my life was incomplete. I was looking for connection. I was always drawn to the Jewish people and our history and particularly to the values that were so easily translated and incorporated into life. It chose me back when at a point I began to interpret those values. Through songs and prayers I was able to reconstruct the same ideas and share them with others.

In your last moments, when you uttered the words "I am a Jew," you gave some people their first experience of acknowledging their Jewish selves. Those who never identified before were awakened by your strength and conviction.

In every interaction—be it a concert, or when I function as a sh'licha tzibur, or at a healing service—in any of my relationships, no matter what I do, I am a Jew. I feel the presence of the Divine and a link to the past. I know there are many who have come before me who have made their mark. They, like you, have left pieces of themselves so that we, the living, might incorporate them into our lives in order to reconstruct the places in our world that have been shattered.

I am a Jew because I know that it is not meant for me to do this work alone. I am engaged both with the Holy One and with all of those with whom I am involved.

I am a Jew because I know the world that you and I and many others like us envision is a world yet to be created by us.

I am a Jew because in spite of all the hatred and violence in this world, I believe we must hope and live together as if the world were sheltered beneath the wings of the Shekhinah. We must live as if we were enveloped in a world of love and compassion.

I am a Jew because together we must pray for the day when all people will sit beneath the vine and fig tree—when none shall be afraid and when all the words that come forth shall be words that speak of the family of humanity.

The world you had envisioned is a world that we will continue to build through song and prayer, through action and acts of loving kindness. Often we dreamers are laughed at for our lofty thoughts. In truth it is love and peace that are two values that cannot be touched or defiled by anyone. They are held in one's heart and soul in the most sacred parts of us, and they soar to the highest heights in the heavens. I had to write you because, though we never met, we were engaged in a shared dream of a world in which all human beings would be seen as precious—to be celebrated and loved.

This piece was not to have been a tribute to you, but it would have been hard to write about "I am a Jew" without making reference to you, since you were and will always be the one who made me think about why I am a Jew. Your memory is a blessing.

CHAPTER

15 Lesson Plan 14

How Does Someone Cope With a Death in the Family?

Gina Berriault, "The Stone Boy"

Lesson 1: Plot-check quiz and discussion of a basic question.
Lesson 2: The movie version of "The Stone Boy" (90 minutes).
Lesson 3: Background on the movie with Gina Berriault and discussion of Gene Siskel's movie review.

1. **Focus:** Journal: Have you ever been disappointed with a movie version of a story that you liked? If so, why so? If not, why not?
2. **Objective:** To resolve a basic question of interpretation on the short story.
3. **Purpose:** To increase our mutual understanding and enjoyment of the original story.
4. **Input:** Begin with a factual plot-check quiz (handout pages 206–207) to check that everyone has read the story. A basic question of interpretation follows on pages 208–209.
5. **Modeling, checking for understanding, guided practice:** During discussion, the teacher (or student co-leaders) *model* the four rules of Socratic discussion and *check for understanding* by asking follow-up questions for clarification, substantiation, consistency, relevance, implication, resolution, and to get more opinion. Guided practice is the discussion.
6. **Closure:** Oral or written resolution (in the journal) of the basic question discussed.

Text: Gina Berriault (1972). "The Stone Boy," *Getting Into Books*. Chicago IL: Great Books Foundation.

Film: *All the Way Home* DVD (107 mins; b/w) (based on the novel *A Death in the Family*).

The Stone Boy

Gina Berriault

Arnold drew his overalls and raveling gray sweater over his naked body. In the other narrow bed his brother Eugene went on sleeping, undisturbed by the alarm clock's rusty ring. Arnold, watching his brother sleeping, felt a peculiar dismay; he was nine, six years younger that Eugie, and in their waking hours it was he who was subordinate. To dispel emphatically his uneasy advantage over his sleeping brother, he threw himself on the hump of Eugie's body.

"Get up! Get up!" he cried.

Arnold felt his brother twist away and saw the blankets lifted in a great wing, and, all in an instant, he was lying on his back under the covers with only his face showing, like a baby and Eugie was sprawled on top of him.

"Whassa matter with you?" asked Eugie in sleepy anger, his face hanging close.

"Get up," Arnold repeated. "You said you'd pick peas with me."

Stupidly, Eugie gazed around the room to see if morning had come into it yet. Arnold began to laugh derisively, making soft, snorting noises, and was thrown off the bed. He got up from the floor and went down the stairs, the laughter continuing like hiccups, against his will. But when he opened the staircase door and entered the parlor, he hunched up his shoulders and was quiet because his parents slept in the bedroom downstairs.

Arnold lifted his .22-caliber rifle from the rack on the kitchen wall. It was an old lever-action that his father had given him because nobody else used it anymore. On their way down to the garden he and Eugie would go by the lake, and if there were any ducks on it he'd take a shot at them. Standing on the stool before the cupboard, he searched on the top shelf in the confusion of medicines and ointments for man and beast and found a small yellow box of .22 cartridges. Then he sat down on the stool and began to load his gun.

It was cold in the kitchen so early, but later in the day, when his mother canned the peas, the heat from the wood stove would be almost unbearable. Yesterday she had finished preserving the huckleberries that the family had picked along the mountain, and before that she had canned all the cherries his father had brought from the warehouse in Corinth. Sometimes, on these summer days, Arnold would deliberately come out from the shade where he was playing and make himself as uncomfortable as his mother was in the kitchen by standing in the sun until the sweat ran down his body.

Eugie came clomping down the stairs and into the kitchen, his head drooping with sleepiness. From his perch on the stool Arnold watched Eugie slip on his green knit cap. Eugie didn't really need a cap; he hadn't had a haircut in a long time and his brown curls grew thick and matted, close around his ears and down his neck, tapering there to a small whorl. Eugie passed his left hand through his hair before he set his cap down with his right. The very way he slipped his cap on was an announcement of his status; almost everything he did was a reminder that he was eldest—first he, then Nora, then Arnold—and called attention to how tall he was, almost as tall as his father, how long his legs were, how small he was in the hips, and what a neat dip above his buttocks his thick-soled logger's boots gave him. Arnold never tired of watching Eugie offer silent praise to himself. He wondered, as he sat enthralled, if when he got to be Eugie's age he would still be undersized and his hair still straight.

Eugie eyed the gun. "Don't you know this ain't duck season?" he asked gruffly, as if he were the sheriff.

"No, I don't know," Arnold said with a snigger.

Eugie picked up the tin washtub for the peas, unbolted the door with his free hand and kicked it open. Then, lifting the tub to his head, he went clomping down the back steps. Arnold followed, closing the door behind him.

The sky was faintly gray, almost white. The mountains behind the farm made the sun climb a long way to show itself. Several miles to the south, where the range opened up, hung an orange mist, but the valley in which the farm lay was still cold and colorless.

Eugie opened the gate to the yard and the boys passed between the barn and the row of chicken houses, their feet stirring up the carpet of brown feathers dropped by the molting chickens. They paused before going down the slope to the lake. A fluky morning wind ran among the shocks of wheat that covered the slope. It sent a shimmer northward across the lake, gently moving the rushes that formed an island in the center. Killdeer, their white markings flashing, skimmed the water, crying their shrill sweet cry. And there at the south end of the lake were four wild ducks, swimming out from the willows into open water.

Arnold followed Eugie down the slope, stealing, as his brother did, from one shock of wheat to another. Eugie paused before climbing through the wire fence that divided the wheat field from the marshy pasture around the lake. They were screened from the ducks by the willows along the lake's edge.

"If you hit your duck, you want me to go in after it?" Eugie said.

"If you want," Arnold said.

Eugie lowered his eyelids, leaving slits of mocking blue. "You'd drown 'fore you got to it, them legs of yours so puny," he said.

He shoved the tub under the fence and, pressing down the center wire, climbed through into the pasture.

Arnold pressed down the bottom wire, thrust a leg through and leaned forward to bring the other leg after. His rifle caught on the wire and he jerked at it. The air was rocked by the sound of a shot. Feeling foolish, he lifted his face, baring it to an expected shower of derision from his brother. But Eugie did not turn around. Instead, from his crouching position, he fell to his knees and then pitched forward onto his face. The ducks rose up crying from the lake, cleared the mountain background and beat away northward across the pale sky.

Arnold squatted beside his brother. Eugie seemed to be climbing the earth, as if the earth ran up and down, and when he found he couldn't scale it he lay still.

"Eugie?"

Then Arnold saw it, under the tendril of hair at the nape of the neck—a slow rising of bright blood. It had an obnoxious movement, like that of a parasite.

"Hey, Eugie," he said again. He was feeling the same discomfort he had felt when he had watched Eugie sleeping; his brother didn't know that he was lying face down in the pasture. Again he said, "Hey, Eugie," an anxious nudge in his voice. But Eugie was still as the morning around them.

Arnold set his rifle on the ground and stood up. He picked up the tub and, dragging it behind him, walked along by the willows to the garden fence and climbed through. He went down on his knees among the tangled vines. The pods were cold with the night, but his hands were strange to him, and not until some time had passed did he realize that the pods were numbing his fingers. He picked from the top of the vine first, then lifted the vine to look underneath for pods, and moved on to the next.

It was a warmth on his back, like a large hand laid firmly there, that made him raise his head. Way up the slope the gray farmhouse was struck by the sun. While his head had been bent the land had grown bright around him.

When he got up his legs were so stiff that he had to go down on his knees again to ease the pain. Then, walking sideways, he dragged the tub, half full of peas, up the slope.

The kitchen was warm now; a fire was roaring in the stove with a closed-up, rushing sound. His mother was spooning eggs from a pot of boiling water and putting them into a bowl. Her short brown hair was uncombed and fell forward across her eyes as she bent her head. Nora was lifting a frying pan full of trout from the stove, holding the handle with a dish towel. His father had just come in from bringing the cows from the north pasture to the barn, and was sitting on the stool, unbuttoning his red plaid Mackinaw.

"Did you boys fill the tub?" his mother asked.

"They ought of by now," his father said. "They went out of the house an hour ago. Eugie woke me up comin' downstairs. I heard you shootin'—did you get a duck?"

"No," Arnold said. They would want to know why Eugie wasn't coming in for breakfast, he thought. "Eugie's dead," he told them.

They stared at him. The pitch crackled in the stove.

"You kids plain' a joke?" his father asked.

"Where's Eugene?" his mother asked scoldingly. She wanted, Arnold knew, to see his eyes, and when he had glanced at her she put the bowl and spoon down on the stove and walked past him. His father stood up and went out the door after her. Nora followed them with little skipping steps, as if afraid to be alone.

Arnold went into the barn, down the foddering passage past the cows waiting to be milked, and climbed into the loft. After a few minutes he heard a terrifying sound coming toward the house. His parents and Nora were returning from the willows, and sounds sharp as knives were rising from his mother's breast and carrying over the sloping fields. In a short while he heard his father go down the back steps, slam the car door and drive away.

Arnold lay still as a fugitive, listening to the cows eating close by. If his parents never called him, he thought he would stay up in the loft forever, out of the way. In the night he would sneak down for a drink of water from the faucet over the trough and for whatever food they left him by the barn.

The rattle of his father's car as it turned down the lane recalled him to the present. He heard the voices of his Uncle Andy and Aunt Alice and they and his father went past the barn to the lake. He could feel the morning growing heavier with sun. Someone, probably Nora, had let the chickens out of their coops and they were cackling in the yard.

After a while another car turned down the road off the highway. The car drew to a stop and he heard the voices of strange men. The men also went past the barn and down to the lake. The undertakers, whom his father must have phoned from Uncle Andy's house, had arrived from Corinth. And then he heard everyone come back and heard the car turn around and leave.

"Arnold!" It was his father calling from the yard.

He climbed down the ladder and went out into the sun, picking wisps of hay from his overalls.

Corinth, nine miles away, was the county seat. Arnold sat in the front of the old Ford between his father, who was driving, and Uncle Andy; no one spoke. Uncle Andy was his mother's brother, and he had been fond of Eugie because Eugie had resembled him. Andy had taken Eugie hunting and had given him a knife and a lot of things, and now Andy, his eyes narrowed, sat tall and stiff beside Arnold.

Arnold's father parked the car before the courthouse. It was a two-story brick building with a lamp on both sides of the bottom step. They went up the wide stone steps, Arnold and his father going first, and entered the darkly paneled hallway. The shirt-sleeved man in the sheriff's office said the sheriff was at Carlson's Parlor examining the Curwing boy.

Andy went off to get the sheriff while Arnold and his father waited on a bench in the corridor. Arnold felt his father watching him, and he lifted his eyes with painful casualness to the announcement, on the opposite wall, of the Corinth County Annual Rodeo, and then to the clock with its loudly clucking pendulum. After he had come down from the loft his father and Uncle Andy had stood in the yard with him and asked him to tell them everything, and he had explained to them how the gun had caught on the wire. But when they had asked him why he hadn't run back to the house to tell his parents, he had had no answer—all he could say was that he had gone down into the garden to pick the peas. His father had stared at him in a pale, puzzled way, and it was then that he had felt his father and the others set their cold, turbulent silence against him. Arnold shifted on the bench, his only feeling a small one of compunction imposed by his father's eyes.

At a quarter past nine Andy and the sheriff came in. They all went into the sheriff's private office, and Arnold was sent forward to sit in the chair by the sheriff's desk; his father and Andy sat down on the bench against the wall.

The sheriff lumped down into his swivel chair and swung toward Arnold. He was an old man with white hair like wheat stubble. His restless green eyes made him seem not to be in his office but to be hurrying and bobbing around somewhere else.

"What did you say your name was?" the sheriff asked.

"Arnold," he replied, but he could not remember telling the sheriff his name before.

"Curwing?"

"Yes."

"What were you doing with a .22, Arnold?"

"It's mine," he said.

"Okay. What were you going to shoot?"

"Some ducks," he replied.

"Out of season?"

He nodded.

"That's bad," said the sheriff. "Were you and your brother good friends?"

What did he mean—good friends? Eugie was his brother. That was different from a friend, Arnold thought. A best friend was your own age, but

Eugie was almost a man. Eugie had had a way of looking at him, slyly and mockingly and yet confidentially, that had summed up how they both felt about being brothers. Arnold had wanted to be with Eugie more than with anybody else but he couldn't say that they had been good friends.

"Did they ever quarrel?" the sheriff asked his father.

"Not that I know," his father replied. "It seemed to me that Arnold cared a lot for Eugie."

"Did you?" the sheriff asked Arnold.

If it seemed so to his father, then it was so. Arnold nodded.

"Were you mad at him this morning?"

"No."

"How did you happen to shoot him?"

"We was crawlin' through the fence."

"Yes?"

"An' the gun got caught on the wire."

"Seems the hammer must of caught," his father put in.

"All right, that's what happened," said the sheriff. "But what I want you to tell me is this. Why didn't you go back to the house and tell your father right away? Why did you go and pick peas for an hour?"

Arnold gazed over his shoulder at his father, expecting his father to have an answer for this also. But his father's eyes, larger and even lighter blue than usual, were fixed upon him curiously. Arnold picked at a callus in his right palm. It seemed odd now that he had not run back to the house and wakened his father, but he could not remember why he had not. They were all waiting for him to answer.

"I come down to pick peas," he said.

"Didn't you think," asked the sheriff stepping carefully from word to word, "that it was more important for you to go tell your parents what had happened?"

"The sun was gonna come up," Arnold said.

"What's that got to do with it?"

"It's better to pick peas while they're cool."

The sheriff swung away from him, laid both hands flat on his desk. "Well, all I can say is," he said across to Arnold's father and Uncle Andy, "he's either a moron or he's so reasonable that he's way ahead of us." He gave a challenging snort. "It's come to my notice that the most reasonable guys are mean ones. They don't feel nothing."

For a moment the three men sat still. Then the sheriff lifted his hand like a man taking an oath. "Take him home," he said.

Andy uncrossed his legs. "You don't want him?"?

"Not now," replied the sheriff. "Maybe in a few years."

Arnold's father stood up. He held his hat against his chest. "The gun ain't his no more," he said wanly.

Arnold went first through the hallway, hearing behind him the heels of his father and Uncle Andy striking the floorboards. He went down the steps ahead of them and climbed into the back seat of the car. Andy paused as he was getting into the front seat and gazed back at Arnold, and Arnold saw that his uncle's eyes had absorbed the knowingness from the sheriff's eyes. Andy and his father and the sheriff had discovered what made him go down into the grain. It was because he was cruel, the sheriff had said, and didn't care about his brother. Arnold lowered his eyelids meekly against his uncle's stare.

The rest of the day he did his tasks around the farm, keeping apart from the family. At evening, when he saw his father stomp tiredly into the house, Arnold did not put down his hammer and leave the chicken coop he was repairing. He was afraid that they did not want him to eat supper with them. But in a few minutes another fear that they would go to the trouble of calling him and that he would be made conspicuous by his tardiness made him follow his father into the house. As he went through the kitchen, he saw the jars of peas standing in rows on the workbench, a reproach to him.

No one spoke at supper, and his mother, who sat next to him, leaned her head in her hand all throughout the meal, curving her fingers over her eyes so as not to see him. They were finishing their small, silent supper when the visitors began to arrive, knocking hard on the back door. The men were coming from their farms now that it was growing dark and they could not work anymore.

Old Man Matthews, gray and stocky, came first, with his two sons, Orion, the elder, and Clint, who was Eugie's age. As the callers entered the parlor where the family ate, Arnold sat down in a rocking chair. Even as he had been undecided before supper whether to remain outside or take his place at the table, he now thought that he should go upstairs, and yet he stayed to avoid being conspicuous by his absence. If he stayed, he thought, as he always stayed and listened when visitors came, they would see that he was only Arnold and not the person the sheriff thought he was. He sat with his arms crossed and his hands tucked into his armpits and did not lift his eyes.

The Matthews men had hardly settled down around the table, after Arnold's mother and Nora had cleared away the dishes, when another car rattled down the road and someone else rapped on the back door. This time it was Sullivan, a spare and sandy man, so nimble of gesture and expression that Arnold had never been able to catch more than a few of his meanings. Sullivan, in dusty jeans, sat down in another rocker, shot out his skinny legs and began to talk in his fast way, recalling everything that Eugene had ever said to him. The other men interrupted to tell of occasions they remembered, and after a time Clint's young voice, hoarse like Eugene's had been, broke in to tell about the time Eugene had beat him in a wrestling match.

Out of the kitchen the voices of Orion's wife and of Mrs. Sullivan mingled with Nora's voice but not, Arnold noticed, with his mother's. Then dry little Mr. Cram came, leaving large Mrs. Cram in the kitchen, and there was no chair left for Mr. Cram to sit in. No one asked Arnold to get up and he was unable to rise. He knew that the story had got around to them during the day about how he had gone and picked peas after he had shot his brother, and he knew that although they were talking only about Eugie they were thinking about him and if he got up, if he moved even his foot, they would all be alerted. Then Uncle Andy arrived and leaned his tall, lanky body against the doorjam and there were two men standing.

Presently Arnold was aware that the talk had stopped. He knew without looking up that the men were watching him.

"Not a tear in his eye," said Andy, and Arnold knew that it was his uncle who had gestured the men to attention.

"He don't give a hoot, is that how it goes?" asked Sullivan, trippingly.

"He's a reasonable fellow," Andy explained. "That's what the sheriff said. It's us who ain't reasonable. If we'd of shot our brother, we'd of come runnin' back to the house, cryin' like a baby. Well, we'd of been unreasonable. What would of been the use of actin' like that? If your brother is shot dead, he's shot dead. What's the use of getting' emotional about it? The thing to do is go down to the garden to pick peas. Am I right?"

The men around the room shifted their heavy, satisfying weight of unreasonableness.

Matthew's son Orion said: "If I'd of done what he done, Pa would've hung my pelt by the side of the big coyote's in the barn."

Arnold sat in the rocker until the last man filed out. While his family was out in the kitchen bidding the callers good night and the cars were driving away down the dirt lane to the highway, he picked up one of the kerosene lamps and slipped quickly up the stairs. In his room he undressed by lamplight, although he and Eugie had always undressed in the dark, and not until he was lying in his bed did he blow out the flame. He felt nothing, not any grief. There was only the same immense silence and crawling inside of him; it was the way the house and fields felt under a merciless man.

He awoke suddenly. He knew that his father was out in the yard, closing the doors of the chicken houses. The sound that had wakened him was the step of his father as he got up from the rocker and went down the back steps. And he knew that his mother was awake in her bed.

Throwing off the covers, he rose swiftly, went down the stairs and across the dark parlor to his parent's room. He rapped on the door.

"Mother?"

From the closed room her voice rose to him, a seeking and retreating voice. "Yes?"

"Mother?" he asked insistently. He had expected her to realize that he wanted to go down on his knees by her bed and tell her that Eugie was dead. She did not know it yet, nobody knew it, and yet she was sitting up in bed, waiting to be told, waiting for him to confirm her dread. He had expected her to tell him to come in, to allow him to dig his head into her blankets and tell her about the terror he had felt when he had knelt beside Eugie. He had come to clasp her in his arms and, in his terror, to pommel her breasts with his head. He put his hand upon the knob.

"Go back to bed, Arnold," she called sharply.

But he waited.

"Go back! Is night when you get afraid?"

At first he did not understand. Then, silently, he left the door and for a stricken moment stood by the rocker. Outside everything was still. The fences, the shocks of wheat seen through the window before him were so still it was as if they moved and breathed in the daytime and had fallen silent with the lateness of the hour. It was a silence that seemed to observe his father, a figure moving alone around the yard, his lantern casting a circle of light by his feet. In a few minutes his father would enter the dark house, the lantern still lighting his way.

Arnold was suddenly aware that he was naked. He had thrown off his blankets and come down the stairs to tell his mother how he felt about Eugie, but she had refused to listen to him and his nakedness had become unpardonable. At once he went back up the stairs, fleeing from his father's lantern.

At breakfast he kept his eyelids lowered as if to deny the humiliating nights. Nora, sitting at his left, did not pass the pitcher of milk to him and he did not ask for it. He would never again, he vowed, ask them for anything, and he ate his fried eggs and potatoes only because everybody ate meals—the cattle ate, and the cats; it was customary for everybody to eat.

"Nora, you gonna keep that pitcher for yourself?" his father asked.

Nora lowered her head unsurely.

"Pass it on to Arnold," his father said.

Nora put her hands in her lap.

His father picked up the metal pitcher and set it down at Arnold's plate.

Arnold, pretending to be deaf to the discord, did not glance up, but relief rained over his shoulders at the thought that his parents recognized him again. They must have lain awake after his father had come in from the yard: had they realized together why he had come down the stairs and knocked on their door?

"Bessie's missin' this morning," his father called out to his mother, who had gone into the kitchen. "She went up the mountain last night and had her calf, most likely. Somebody's got to go up and find her 'fore the coyotes get the calf."

That had been Eugie's job, Arnold thought. Eugie would climb the cattle trails in search of a newborn calf and come down the mountain carrying the calf across his back, with the cow running behind him, mooing in alarm.

Arnold ate the few more forkfuls of his breakfast, put his hands on the edge of the table and pushed back his chair. If he went for the calf he'd be away from the farm all morning. He could switch the cow down the mountain slowly, and the calf would run along at its mother's side.

When he passed through the kitchen his mother was setting a kettle of water on the stove.

"Where you going?" she asked awkwardly.

"Up to get the calf," he replied, averting his face.

"Arnold?"

At the door he paused reluctantly, his back to her, knowing that she was seeking him out, as his father was doing, and he called upon his pride to protect him from them.

"Was you knocking at my door last night?"

He looked over his shoulder at her, his eyes narrow and dry.

"What'd you want?" she asked humbly.

"I didn't want nothing," he said flatly.

Then he went out the door and down the back steps, his legs trembling from the fright his answer gave him.

"The Stone Boy" by Gina Berriault

PLOT-CHECK QUIZ

Directions: On your own paper, next to each number, write a short answer to complete this plot summary of the story.

As the story begins, the Curwing brothers, Arnold and Eugene set out in early morning to (1) ____________________ . Arnold, who is (2) ________________ years old, idolizes his older brother who is (3) __________________ years old. Arnold wonders if when he reached Eugene's age he would still be (4) ______________.As the boys leave the farmhouse, (5) __________________ brings along his (6) _______________ in hopes that he might (7) _____________ _______________. But before they can get to work, a terrible accident (8) ______________________________ occurs. Strangely, after the accident, Arnold does not (9) ____________________________ but rather (10) ______________.

When Arnold returns to the farmhouse, he says only that (11) __________________. At first, his parents think he is (12) ______________. Soon, however, they discover the awful truth that (13) __________________. Because of Arnold's behavior—(14) ____________________________—many problems arise for him. For example, he becomes (15) ________________________; as a result, he becomes the film's title character.

Arnold's father and (16) ________________________, who favors Eugene because (17) ____________________, take Arnold to Corinth to be questioned by the sheriff. After the sheriff asks if Arnold had been friends with Eugene or if he had been (18) _____________ with him, he then asks the all-important question about (19) ________________________________. In reply, Arnold says only that (20) ____________________. The sheriff then comments that Arnold is "either a (21) _______________ or he's so (22) _______________ that he's way ahead of us."

After Arnold returns to the farmhouse, visitors arrive who begin to (23) ______________________________ for his behavior after Eugene's death. That night Arnold wants to speak with his mother but she turns him away because she is too (24) ____________________ to hear his confession of grief. In the morning after she realizes what she has done to hurt her son, she asks Arnold what he wanted the night before. He replies flatly, "I didn't want (25) _________________." Then he walks out the door and down the back steps. He legs tremble from the (26) _________________ his answer gave him.

Socratic Seminar 1

Basic Question 1: Why do none of the adults in the story understand what Arnold has gone through in killing his brother?

1. Why is Uncle Andy surprised that the sheriff lets Arnold return home after questioning him?
2. What does the sheriff mean when he says in Arnold's presence, "he's either a moron or he's so reasonable that he's way ahead of us"?
3. Why does Arnold's mother refuse to let him come into her bedroom on the night of Eugene's death?
4. Does Arnold's father fail to understand Arnold's grief because his son can offer no reasonable explanation for not running back to the house for help?
5. Why does Berriault reveal to readers the depth of Arnold's grief while none of the adult are able to perceive it?
6. Does Arnold become a stone boy chiefly because none of the adults were able to understand his lack of evident emotion at the loss of his brother?
7. After Uncle Andy's comment during the wake shaming Arnold for his lack of a show of emotion, why does the narrator say, "The men around the room shifted their heavy, satisfying weight of unreasonableness"?
8. When the author ends her story with Arnold's reply to his mother's question that he didn't want anything, is Berriault implying that his parents have lost two sons?

Socratic Seminar 2

James Agee's posthumously published Pulitzer Prize-winning novel, *A Death in the Family* is set in Knoxville, TN, in 1915. The death of husband and father Jay Follett (John Slattery) in a car accident has profound and long-reaching effects upon his wife, Mary (Annabeth Gish), and his sensitive, six-year-old son, Rufus (Austin Wolff). At the core of the crisis is Mary's prickly relationship with her own family, exacerbated by her late husband's unwillingness to "go with the flow" in terms of religion and race relations. The kindly intervention of Mary's free-spirited artist brother, Andrew (David Alford) enables her and her son to go on with their lives. Told from Rufus' point of view, the novel version of *A Death in the Family* had previously served as the source for the Broadway play and film *All the Way Home* DVD 1963 (97 mins; b/w). This production, filmed on location in Tennessee, was telecast by PBS on March 25, 2002 as part of Masterpiece Theatre's "American Collection."

A Death in the Family Part III, Chapters 14–16

Assignment: For discussion, write five related interpretive follow-up questions for each assigned basic question of interpretation. Include a page reference for each question. For example:

Basic Question 2: How do Rufus and Catherine cope with the sudden death of their father?

Does their mother Mary enable the children to understand why God has called their father to Himself? (page 227)

Basic Question 3: Why does Rufus reject their Mother's and Aunt Hanna's explanation that his father died because God wanted him to be with Him?

Why is Rufus able to get Aunt Hanna to admit that a concussion, "Not God," killed his father? (237–238)

Basic Question 4: Why does Rufus feel so guilty about telling his classmates "My Daddy's dead"?

At his chair, why does Rufus tell his father, "I didn't mean to do bad"? (255)

A Death in the Family Part III, Chapters 17–20

Basic Question 5: How does Uncle Andrew help Rufus cope with the sudden death of his father?

Why does Uncle Andrew tell Rufus that he thought of his father as a great man as Lincoln had been? (276)

Basic Question 6: Why does Uncle Andrew tell Rufus that the miraculous butterfly has "more of God in him than that priggish, mealy-mouthed son of a bitch [Father Jackson]?

Why is Rufus glad that his uncle did not like Father Jackson and wished that his mother did not like him either? (308)

Basic Question 7: Why does Agee reveal that Rufus understands more about his father's death than what he is told?

Why does Agee end his novel with Rufus and his uncle walking "all the way home in silence"?

Nonfiction Readings: An Interview with Gina Berriault

When asked about her inspiration for the film version of "The Stone Boy," Gina Berriault replied "The idea for the story came from a news item about a hunting accident; and at the time I read it, I was living for the summer on a farm in Montana, and that is where I set the story . . . But I make up all the persons in the story . . . It is an original idea."

Was she pleased with her screenplay? "Not really. I was ultimately disappointed in the way that the film turned out." She explained that the screenplay was her attempt to answer the question that students most frequently asked her, "What's going to happen to Arnold?"

1. Given this background information, what do students think it was that made Berriault dissatisfied with her screenplay? (The interviewer did not follow up to ask her to explain her disappointment.)
2. How does the movie try to link to two plots—the plot of the original short story (Arnold's rejection by adults) and the plot of the screenplay (the demise of Uncle Andy and Lucille's marriage)?
3. Which, if any, of the connections between the two plots are plausible? For example, why did Arnold go to Reno to apologize to his aunt Lucille?

"Sympathetic Relationship Heals 'Stone Boy' Wounds": Mini-Review

Gene Siskel, *Chicago Tribune*, Thursday, April 26, 1984

"Silence is not always golden"

The cast

Joe Hillerman	Robert Duvall
Andy Jensen	Frederic Forrest
Ruth Hillerman	Glenn Close
George Jensen	Wilford Brimley
Arnold Hillerman	Jason Presson
Lu Jensen	Gail Youngs
Amalie	Cindy Fisher
Nora Hillerman	Susan Blackstone
Eugene Hillerman	Dean Cain

1. If you are excited at the prospect of seeing another Robert Duvall film, you probably will be disappointed with "The Stone Boy." It's not anything that Duvall does; it's what he doesn't do. Even though he receives top billing, his role is one of the smallest in the film. He spends most of his time staring off into the darkness, his back to the camera. Making a similarly limited impression is Glen Close, playing his wife. Indeed, theirs is not the central relationship in this purposefully noncommercial movie.
2. Rather, at the center of "The Stone Boy" is the relationship between a traumatized child and his sensitive, loving grandfather, played by Wilford Brimley, a superb character actor who has his best role in this film. "The Stone Boy" is a drama of silence and communication built upon a tragedy. Set in the big sky country of Montana, "The Stone Boy" opens with two boys, one 12 years old, the other a few years older, leaving their farmhouse to go pick peas.
3. The younger brother has brought along his gun, hoping to bag a wild duck, but before they get to work, a terrible accident occurs. As the boys climb through a fence, the gun gets caught on a wire. Trying to free it, the younger brother accidentally causes the gun to fire, killing his older brother.
4. It's one of those moments that seems both small and monumental. A bullet passes through a body and snuffs out a life. It doesn't seem right that something that small can do so much damage. Those, though, are the thoughts of an adult. No one knows what goes through the mind of twelve-year-old Arnold Hillerman [played by Jason Presson] as he stands in the field, feeling responsible for his brother's death. Instead of running to tell his parents, Arnold stays in the field for some time and in some kind of twisted way to deny what's happened, he begins to pick peas.
5. The delay means nothing, because his brother is dead. But later that delay, that denial, will cause more problems for Arnold, who in silent suffering becomes the film's title character. The rest of "The Stone Boy" follows the forces that keep Arnold in his shell and those that work to free him and his family of their curse of resentment and silence. It's a journey in search of a way to come back from being dead while alive, and the character of the grandfather holds the key. The boys' father and mother [Duvall and Close] are too distraught to heal their own son.
6. "The Stone Boy" would be a more commercial film if it narrowed its focus to these four characters: the father, mother, son, and grandfather. But in what may turn out to be a fatal box-office decision, the story has

been enlarged to include sizable roles for Close's philandering brother [Frederic Forrest] and his put-upon wife. These two characters rail at each other throughout the movie to no great purpose.

7. The Academy Award-winning Duvall has already received ample praise for his past many achievements. So let us now praise Wilford Brimley. There is a quiet power within Brimley that results from his just being there. He comes across as a person who has lived a lot of years and seen a lot of things and probably knows a things or two about life. That describes every character Brimley has played, and those qualities are desperately needed by his grandson in "The Stone Boy." Someone in this family has to reach out and make a connection to this hurting boy.
8. "The Stone Boy" tells the story at a labored pace, not giving in to easy, cathartic drama. That makes it less commercial and a bit frustrating at times to sit through. Nevertheless, "The Stone Boy" reveals in detail the work that goes into the art of healing, and that is a subject foreign to most American movies. For that reason, "The Stone Boy" is recommended.

"Sympathetic Relationship Heals 'Stone Boy' Wounds" by Gene Siskel

Directions: As you read Siskel's movie review make notations and then answer these questions in complete sentences in your journal.

Before *viewing the movie version*:

1. Why does Siskel think we will be disappointed with the movie version of Gina Berriault's story?
2. Why does Siskel think that Arnold picked peas after his brother's death?
3. Based on your reading of the original story, do you agree with Siskel's interpretation of Arnold's behavior after Eugene's death? If so, why so? If not, why not?
4. In the original story, why does no one reach out to help Arnold cope with the loss of his brother?
5. What is Siskel's chief objection to the movie?
6. In spite of his objections, why does Siskel still recommend the movie?
7. Explain how, specifically, Siskel's movie review is a model of good writing.

After *viewing the movie version*:

8. Unlike the short story, why does the movie concentrate not on Arnold's growing isolation but on the sympathetic relationship between Arnold and his loving grandfather?
9. Do you agree with Siskel that "the philandering brother" [uncle Andy] of Arnold's mother [Ruth] and his "put-upon wife" [Lucille] rail at each other for no dramatic purpose? If so, why so? If not, why not?
10. Unlike the movie, does the short story imply that the Curwings have lost two sons? If so, why so? If not, why not?
11. List three specific changes *that you liked* in the movie.
12. List three specific changes *that you disliked* in the movie.

Nonfiction Reading

The following is the full transcript text of President Obama's speech at the Sandy Hook Interfaith Prayer Vigil in Newtown, Connecticut, on December 16, 2012.

"In the Face of Unconscionable Evil"

Thank you. Thank you, Governor. To all the families, first responders, to the community of Newtown, clergy, guests—Scripture tells us: ". . . do not lose heart. Though outwardly we are wasting away . . . inwardly we are being renewed day by day. For our light and momentary troubles are achieving for us an eternal glory that far outweighs them all. So we fix our eyes not on what is seen, but on what is unseen, since what is seen is temporary, but what is unseen is eternal. For we know that if the earthly tent we live in is destroyed, we have a building from God, an eternal house in heaven, not built by human hands." (2 Cor 4:16–5:1)

We gather here in memory of twenty beautiful children and six remarkable adults. They lost their lives in a school that could have been any school; in a quiet town full of good and decent people that could be any town in America.

Here in Newtown, I come to offer the love and prayers of a nation. I am very mindful that mere words cannot match the depths of your sorrow, nor can they heal your wounded hearts. I can only hope it helps for you to know that you're not alone in your grief; that our world too has been torn apart; that all across this land of ours, we have wept with you, we've pulled our children tight. And you must know that whatever measure of comfort we can provide, we will provide; whatever portion of sadness that we can share with you to ease this heavy load, we will gladly bear it. Newtown—you are not alone.

As these difficult days have unfolded, you've also inspired us with stories of strength and resolve and sacrifice. We know that when danger arrived in the halls of Sandy Hook Elementary, the school's staff did not flinch, they did not hesitate. Dawn Hochsprung and Mary Sherlach, Vicki Soto, Lauren Rousseau, Rachel Davino and Anne Marie Murphy—they responded as we all hope we might respond in such terrifying circumstances—with courage and with love, giving their lives to protect the children in their care.

We know that there were other teachers who barricaded themselves inside classrooms, and kept steady through it all, and reassured their students by saying "wait for the good guys, they're coming"; "show me your smile."

And we know that good guys came. The first responders who raced to the scene, helping to guide those in harm's way to safety, and comfort those in need, holding at bay their own shock and trauma because they had a job to do, and others needed them more.

And then there were the scenes of the schoolchildren, helping one another, holding each other, dutifully following instructions in the way that young children sometimes do; one child even trying to encourage a grown-up by saying, "I know karate. So it's okay. I'll lead the way out." (Laughter.) As a community, you've inspired us, Newtown. In the face of indescribable violence, in the face of unconscionable evil, you've looked out for each other, and you've cared for one another and you've loved one another. This is how Newtown will be remembered. And with time, and God's grace, that love will see you through.

But we, as a nation, we are left with some hard questions. Someone once described the joy and anxiety of parenthood as the equivalent of having your heart outside of your body all the time, walking around. With their very first cry, this most precious, vital part of ourselves—our child—is suddenly exposed to the world, to possible mishap or malice. And every parent knows there is nothing we will not do to shield our children from harm. And yet, we also know that with that child's very first step, and each step after that, they are separating from us; that we won't—that we can't—always be there for them. They'll suffer sickness and setbacks and broken hearts and disappointments. And we learn that our most important job is to give them what they need to become self-reliant and capable and resilient, ready to face the world without fear.

And we know we can't do this by ourselves. It comes as a shock at a certain point where you realize, no matter how much you love these kids, you can't do it by yourself. That this job of keeping our children safe, and teaching them well, is something we can only do together, with the help of friends and neighbors, the help of a community, and the help of a nation. And in that way, we come to realize that we bear a responsibility for every child because we're counting on everybody else to help look after ours; that we're all parents; that they're all our children.

This is our first task—caring for our children. It's our first job. If we don't get that right, we don't get anything right. That's how, as a society, we will be judged.

And by that measure, can we truly say, as a nation, that we are meeting our obligations? Can we honestly say that we're doing enough to keep our children—all of them—safe from harm? Can we claim, as a nation, that we're all together there, letting them know that they are loved, and teaching them to love in return? Can we say that we're truly doing enough to give all the children of this country the chance they deserve to live out their lives in happiness and with purpose?

I've been reflecting on this the last few days, and if we're honest with ourselves, the answer is no. We're not doing enough. And we will have to change.

Since I've been President, this is the fourth time we have come together to comfort a grieving community torn apart by a mass shooting. The fourth time we've hugged survivors. The fourth time we've consoled the families of victims. And in between, there have been an endless series of deadly shootings across the country, almost daily reports of victims, many of them children, in small towns and big cities all across America—victims whose—much of the time, their only fault was being in the wrong place at the wrong time.

We can't tolerate this anymore. These tragedies must end. And to end them, we must change. We will be told that the causes of such violence are complex, and that is true. No single law—no set of laws can eliminate evil from the world, or prevent every senseless act of violence in our society.

But that can't be an excuse for inaction. Surely, we can do better than this. If there is even one step we can take to save another child, or another parent, or another town, from the grief that has visited Tucson, and Aurora, and Oak Creek, and Newtown, and communities from Columbine to Blacksburg before that—then surely we have an obligation to try.

In the coming weeks, I will use whatever power this office holds to engage my fellow citizens—from law enforcement to mental health professionals to parents and educators—in an effort aimed at preventing more tragedies like this. Because what choice do we have? We can't accept events like this as routine. Are we really prepared to say that we're powerless in the face of such carnage, that the politics are too hard? Are we prepared to say that such violence visited on our children year after year after year is somehow the price of our freedom?

All the world's religions—so many of them represented here today—start with a simple question: Why are we here? What gives our life meaning? What gives our acts purpose? We know our time on this Earth is fleeting. We know that we will each have our share of pleasure and pain; that even after we chase after some earthly goal, whether it's wealth or power or fame, or just simple comfort, we will, in some fashion, fall short of what we had hoped. We know that no matter how good our intentions, we will all stumble sometimes, in some way. We will make mistakes, we will experience hardships. And even when we're trying to do the right thing, we know that much of our time will be spent groping through the darkness, so often unable to discern God's heavenly plans.

There's only one thing we can be sure of, and that is the love that we have—for our children, for our families, for each other. The warmth of a small child's embrace—that is true. The memories we have of them, the joy that they bring, the wonder we see through their eyes, that fierce and boundless love we feel for them, a love that takes us out of ourselves, and binds us to something larger—we know that's what matters. We know we're always doing right when we're taking care of them, when we're teaching them well, when we're showing acts of kindness. We don't go wrong when we do that.

That's what we can be sure of. And that's what you, the people of Newtown, have reminded us. That's how you've inspired us. You remind us what matters. And that's what should drive us forward in everything we do, for as long as God sees fit to keep us on this Earth.

"Let the little children come to me," Jesus said, "and do not hinder them—for to such belongs the kingdom of heaven." (Lk 18:16, Mt 19:14, Mk 19:14)

"It is impossible that scandals should not come; but woe to him by whom they come. It would be better for him that a millstone were hanged about his neck, and cast into the sea than that he should scandalize one of these little children." (Lk 17:2)

"Unless you become as little children, you shall not enter the Kingdom of Heaven." (Mt 18:3)

Charlotte. Daniel. Olivia. Josephine. Ana. Dylan. Madeleine. Catherine. Chase. Jesse. James. Grace. Emilie. Jack. Noah. Caroline. Jessica. Benjamin. Avielle. Allison.

God has called them all home.* For those of us who remain, let us find the strength to carry on, and make our country worthy of their memory.

May God bless and keep those we've lost in His heavenly place.

May He grace those we still have with His holy comfort.

And may He bless and watch over this community, and the United States of America.

*Editorial note: To hold God responsible is bad theology. God did not call these children Home. On the contrary, a madman sent them Home.

Afterword

"In a common core curriculum, what is the value of studying 'the best that is known and thought in the world'?"

Victor J. Moeller

The Zebra Storyteller

Spencer Holst

Once upon a time there was a Siamese cat who pretended to be a lion and spoke inappropriate Zebraic.

That language is whinnied by the race of striped horses in Africa.

Here now: An innocent zebra is walking in a jungle and approaching from another direction is the little cat; they meet.

"Hello there!" says the Siamese cat in perfectly pronounced Zebraic. "It certainly is a pleasant day, isn't it? The sun is shining, the birds are singing; isn't the world a lovely place to live today?"

The zebra is so astonished at hearing a Siamese cat speaking like a zebra, why—he's fit to be tied.

So the little cat quickly ties him up, kills him, and drags the better parts of the carcass back to his den.

The cat successfully hunted zebras many months in this manner, dining on filet mignon of zebra every night, and from the better hides he made bow ties and wide belts after the fashion of the decadent princes of the Old Siamese court.

He began boasting to his friends he was a lion, and he gave them as proof the fact that he hunted zebras.

The delicate noses of the zebras told them there was really no lion in the neighborhood. The zebra deaths caused many to avoid the region. Superstitious, they decided the woods were haunted by the ghost of a lion.

One day the storyteller of the zebras was ambling, and through his mind ran plots for stories to amuse the other zebras, when suddenly he eyes brightened, and he said, "That's it! I'll tell a story about a Siamese cat who learns to speak our language! What an idea! That'll make 'em laugh!"

Just then the Siamese cat appeared before him, and said, "Hello there! Pleasant day today, isn't it?"

The zebra storyteller wasn't fit to be tied at hearing a cat speaking his language, because he'd been thinking about that very thing.

He took a good look at the cat, and he didn't know what, but there was something about his looks he didn't like, so he kicked him with a hoof and killed him.

That is the function of a storyteller.

Matthew Arnold's question about Great Books deserves an answer. The most obvious reason has to be that stories are **entertaining** and amusing. With imaginative literature, there is something to satisfy everyone's taste—from romance, to gothic tales, to mystery, to westerns, to science-fiction, to whatever! Look around. Be a browser. Talk to a reader.

Reading stories also **educates our imaginations.** Those who think that a story like "The Zebra Storyteller" (see text) is dumb or stupid, have not developed their imaginations. In fiction, anything can happen and an author does not have to prove anything. Our only obligation as readers is to understand the world that an author has placed us in—not to argue about the author's creation. If we do so, we can increase our enjoyment immensely. Unless we develop our imaginations, we will remain literal-minded and foolishly demand that all stories be true-to-life. How dull that would be.

On the other hand, the contrast between the real or actual and the extraordinary or the fanciful, suggests two different uses that readers make of imaginative literature. Sometimes we **do** want to read about people like ourselves, or about places, things, experiences, and ideas that we are familiar with and make us feel comfortable. In the process of reading about situations related to our own lives, **we can learn more about ourselves and the world about us.** Realism will always have its appeal.

But at other times, the last thing that we want is a story about people like ourselves or experiences similar to those in our everyday lives. We might be accused of wanting **to escape.** We want something **different or strange**—like Stephen King stories. We want to get out of ourselves and the confining, all-too-familiar, and learn that there are other ways of looking at the world besides our own. In short, we want to read about exotic places, about other worlds that have never existed, or worlds that may never exist. The romantic spirit will always contend with realism's appeal.

Stories also prepare us for the unexpected and help us **to avoid projecting false hopes and fears** (such as superstitious zebras who think that they are being preyed on by the ghosts of lions) and show us what we can actually expect in our everyday lives. Because some people never train their imagination to project any other "story" than their own, they cannot conceive of any other shape for their expectations. As a result, they remain stunted and naive about life.

Reading stories can also put us **in closer touch with our feelings**. Good stories, powerful stories, **revulse us** at what is ugly and cruel and mean in life. On the other hand, stories can also **inspire us** to marvel at what is good and wonderful and beautiful in life. Recall George's devotion to Lennie in *Of Mice and Men*, or in *The Great Gatsby*, Nick Carraway's refusal to become as self-serving as those about him. In short, some stories can be so terrible that they may move us to tears and prompt us to say, "That's the way life must never be," while others are so poignant that we find ourselves saying, "That's the way life ought to be," or, "That's the way life could be!"

Most importantly and most profoundly, reading enables us to grasp our identity, **our own personal narratives** because it requires us to overcome our infinite capacity for distraction and our culture of the present now which too many think demands or deserves immediate attention and response. In short, reflective, active, and close reading of good literature, of great books, enables us to discover our own narrative—who we are and who we want to be.

References

Adler, Mortimer J. (1940). "How to Mark a Book." *The Saturday Review* (July 6).

Adler, Mortimer J. (1940). *How To Read a Book: The Art of Getting a Liberal Education.* New York: Simon & Schuster.

Adler, Mortimer J. (1955). *A Guide for Leaders of Great Books Discussion Groups.* Chicago: Great Books Foundation.

Adler, Mortimer J. (1977). *Reforming Education: Opening the American Mind.* New York: MacMillan.

Adler, Mortimer J. (1981). *Six Great Ideas.* New York: MacMillan.

Adler, Mortimer J. (1982). *The Paidea Proposal.* New York: MacMillan.

Adler, Mortimer J. (1983). *Paidea Problems and Possibilities.* New York: MacMillan.

Adler, Mortimer J. (1984). *The Paidea Program.* New York: MacMillan.

Barthes, R. (1975). *The Pleasure of the Text.* New York: Hill and Wang.

Berriault, G. (1972). "The Stone Boy," *Getting Into Books.* Chicago IL: Great Books Foundation.

Bloom, B. (Ed.). (1956). *Taxonomy of Educational Objectives*: Cognitive Domain. New York: McKay.

Bloom, H. (2000). *How to Read and Why.* New York: Scribner.

Bruner, J. (1960). *The Process of Education.* New York: Alfred A. Knopf.

Burke, J. (2010). *What's the Big Idea: Question Driven Teaching Units.* Portsmouth, NH: Heinemann.

Dewey, J. (1997). *How We Think.* Mineola, NY: Dover Publications.

Frye, N. (1970). *The Educated Imagination.* Bloomington, IN: Indiana University Press.

Glaspey, Terry. (2001). *Great Reading: A Guided Tour of Classic and Contemporary Literature.* Downers Grove, IL: InterVarsity Press.

Holst, S. (1993). *The Zebra Storyteller: Collected Stories.* Barrytown, NY: Station Hill Press.

Hutchins, R. M. (1952). *The Great Conversation.* Vol. 1 of Great Books of the Western World. Chicago, IL: Encyclopedia Britannica.

Jacobs, Alan. (2001). *A Theology of Reading: The Hermeneutics of Love.* Boulder, CO: Westview Press.

Jacobs, Alan. (2011). *The Pleasures of Reading in an Age of Distraction.* New York: Oxford University Press; Boulder, CO: Westview Press.

Kreeft, Peter. (2002). *Socrates Meets Jesus.* Downers Grove, IL: InterVarsity Press.

Kutz, E., and Roskelly, H. (1991). *An Unquiet Pedagogy: Transforming Practice in the English Classroom.* Portsmouth, NH: Boynton/Cook.

Mann, T. (1969). *The Magic Mountain.* New York: Alfred A. Knopf, Vintage Books Edition.

McCullers, C. (1987). "Sucker," *Collected Stories.* New York: Houghton Mifflin Co.

Monaco, James. (2000). *How to Read a Film: The World of Movies & Media.* New York: Oxford University Press.

Phillips, Christopher. (2001). *Socrates Cafe: A Fresh Taste of Philosophy.* New York: Norton & Co.

Phillips, Christopher. (2004). *Six Questions of Socrates.* New York: Norton & Co.

Postman, N. (1985). *Amusing Ourselves to Death: Public Discourse in the Age of Show Business.* New York: Penguin Group.

Quindlen, Anna. (1998). *How Reading Changed My Life.* New York: Ballatine Books.

Richards, I. A. (1942). *How to Read* [reap] *a Page: A Course in Efficient Reading.* Boston, MA: Beacon Press.

Roberts, T. (1999). *The Paideia Classroom: Teaching for Understanding.* Larchmont, NY: Eye on Education.

Rosenblatt, Louise. (1968). *Literature as Exploration.* New York: Noble and Noble.

Rosenblatt, Louise. (1978). *The Reader, the Text, and the Poem.* Carbondale, IL: Southern Illinois University Press.

Rouse, W. H. (1995). *The Great Dialogues of Plato.* New York: Signet Classics.

Sanders, Norris. (1966). *Classroom Questions: What Kinds?* New York: Harper & Row.

Saroyan, W. (1958). *The William Saroyan Reader.* New York: Barricade Books, Inc.

Saroyan, W. (1948). *Saroyan Special: Selected Short Stories.* New York: Harcourt Brace & Co.

Saroyan, W. (1962). "Gaston," *The Atlantic Monthly*, February 1962. Published as a book in 1963.

Teasley, Alan B., and Wilder, Ann. (1997). *Reel Conversations: Reading Films with Young Adults.* Portsmouth, NH: Boynton/Cook.

Ulin, David. (2010). *The Lost Art of Reading: Why Books Matter in a Distracted Time.* Seattle, WA: Sasquatch Books.

Warren, R. and Wellek, W. (1956). *Theory of Literature.* New York: Harcourt: Brace & Company.

Whitehead, A. N. (1929). *The Aims of Education.* New York: Macmillan Co.

Printed by PGSTL